WHY DOES *Santa* WEAR RED?

. . . and 100 Other Christmas
Curiosities Unwrapped

MEERA LESTER

△adamsmedia
Avon, Massachusetts

Published by Adams Media, an F+W Publications Company
57 Littlefield Street
Avon, MA 02322
www.adamsmedia.com

ISBN-10: 1-59869-457-X
ISBN-13: 978-1-59869-457-4

Library of Congress Cataloging-in-Publication Data
Lester, Meera.
  Why does santa wear red? / Meera Lester.
    p.   cm.
  ISBN-13: 978-1-59869-457-4 (pbk.)
  ISBN-10: 1-59869-457-X (pbk.)
  1. Christmas. 2. Christmas decorations. 3. Christmas
cookery. I. Title.
  GT4985.L465 2007
  394.2663—dc22   2007018999

Printed in Canada.

J I H G F E D C B A

Interior images © istockphoto.com

This book is available at quantity discounts for bulk purchases.
For information, please call 1-800-289-0963.

CONTENTS

Part 5: Santa: A Man of Myth, Reality, and Mispronunciation

Part 6: Deck the Halls

WHY DOES *Santa* WEAR RED?

Part 7: All the Little Things We Do

Part 8: Crafty Gifts for All to Make

Part 9: Giving and Receiving

Part 10: A Pop-Culture Christmas

Part 11: Sugar Plums Dancing: Recipes for the Season

Part 12: A Literary Look at Christmas

Part 13: Christmas, a Poet's Pastime

INTRODUCTION

Many of us understand the basic stuff about Christmas. Most of us know, for example, that Christmas is the celebration of the birthday of Jesus. But how do we know if he was really born on December 25? And how about those wise men? Who were those guys, and where did they come from? Was it really a star or some other cosmic event that guided them? Maybe you are like me and have an insatiable curiosity about this special holiday. Perhaps you have children and have been the target of a few million questions yourself. Most of their questions are about the guy in the red suit and what he carries in his sleigh. You've probably answered the best you can, but what do you tell them when they ask how the reindeer keep from sliding right off a snow-covered roof? Do people on hot Caribbean islands have chimneys? How many names does Santa have? When did Mrs. Claus emerge from obscurity? What is wassailing, anyway?

With enough questions to fill Santa's toy sack, what we all need are answers. I admit that I didn't interview Santa or Mrs. Claus for this book (who'd know that they go on vacation, too?), but I did do a lot of research and am eager to share it with you. So make yourself a cup of cocoa, put your feet up, and get ready to take a magical sleigh ride through Christmas with me.

part one

the first christmas

*T*he first Christmas must have been awesome to behold. A light brighter than anyone had ever known moved across the night sky to guide wise men from the East to Bethlehem, birthplace of the newborn king. They found him swaddled in cloth and lying in a manger. Next to baby was his mother Mary, undoubtedly exhausted from giving birth, and Joseph, her betrothed, by her side. As the wise men bowed to pay homage to Jesus and offer their gifts, maybe they felt a mystical energy. Perhaps they saw an effulgent light encircling the baby and his parents. Because the only eyewitnesses to the event were the wise men, the Holy Family, and the angels on high, we will never know. Luckily the story of the first Christmas has inspired the imagination of artists, authors, poets, and musicians for centuries—and everyone can appreciate their interpretations. Let's take a look at this inspiring story.

WHY DOES *Santa* WEAR RED?

WHEN IS JESUS' ACTUAL BIRTHDAY? Although Christmas Day is the holiday that celebrates the birth of Christ, and tradition marks the date as December 25, it is not a date that appears in the Bible. In fact, the New Testament does not give the precise date when Jesus was born. The two gospels that shed light on Jesus' birth are Matthew and Luke, but their accounts differ and are not easily reconciled. And we're just talking here about the year, not the month and day.

The Gospel of Matthew mentions the "Massacre of the Innocents," or the slaughter of babies two years and younger, during the reign of Herod the Great, which prompted Joseph and Mary to take Jesus and flee from Bethlehem to Egypt. Herod died in 4 B.C., so Jesus was born, according to Matthew, prior to Herod's death.

The Gospel of Luke, however, states that Jesus was born during the time of a Roman census that obliged all taxpayers to register in regions of their ancestral homes. The Jewish historian Josephus wrote that the census took place in A.D. 6, when Quirinius was governor. Jesus' parents were obliged to travel from their home in Nazareth to Bethlehem to be taxed (Luke 2:4). And although Mary was about to deliver, she accompanied Joseph.

Luke's gospel begins with the pregnancy of Elizabeth, cousin of Jesus' mother Mary. Mary and her cousin's pregnancies are closely linked. Mary conceived when Elizabeth was already six months pregnant (Luke 1:36). Luke starts the infancy narrative in the days of Herod the Great, King of Judea (Luke 1:5), so Herod was still alive when Mary was pregnant with Jesus. However, the second chapter of Luke states that the birth of Jesus took place during the pan-Roman census when Quirinius was governor, some ten years after Herod's death. So at best, Luke provides a ten-year range, that is, 4 B.C. to A.D. 6.

✳ Festive Fact ✳

What's so special about late December, though? Well for one thing, it's the part of the year when the days finally begin to get longer.

Figuring out the month and day of Jesus' birth is just as difficult. Many Old Testament prophets were believed to have died on the same day on which they were conceived or born. If this holds true for Jesus, counting forward nine months from the anniversary of his crucifixion on Good Friday, which early Christians believed to be March 25, would put his birth day on December 25 or January 6 (depending on when Good Friday fell in the year determined to be his birth year, which we have discovered is not easy to pinpoint).

An obscure document attributed to Theophilus of Antioch (A.D. 171–183) is one of the earliest known references to December 25 as the date of Jesus' birth. In the second century, Clement of Alexandria, an early church father, and others speculated on other possible dates. Pope Julius 1 settled it when he decreed December 25 as the date of the Christ child's birth. Most churches eventually adopted December 25 as the day to honor the birth of Christ, and that is the day the birth is celebrated throughout the world.

✦

MARY, "ONE OF THE GUYS?" AND THE CENSUS

The Roman census of the "whole world" (meaning the whole Roman Empire) was conducted during Quirinius' tenure as governor of Syria. It required all men to return to their ancestral regions to register. Some sources say that there was no Jewish or Roman requirement for Mary to make that journey. So why did Mary have to go? Her baby was due, and she was not yet Joseph's wife (Luke 2:5). The Gospel of Luke states that the census was undertaken for purposes of taxation. Other references assert that it also may have required a signature as an oath of loyalty to Caesar Augustus, the supreme ruler of the Roman Empire.

The Gospel of Luke states that Joseph "was of the house and lineage of David" (Luke 2:3), potentially a claimant to the royal throne of David and possibly a threat to Rome and her rulers. Herod certainly desired to know the identity of all the potential claimants and required all of those in Judea who were of royal Judaic lineage to register in Bethlehem, the city of David. Some sources state that a Jewish woman could pass along the royal Davidic lineage by way of her offspring and descendants. If this was the reason for or a benefit of the census, then Joseph and Mary surely had to make that trip to Bethlehem. But hold on. If Jesus' birth occurred in 4 B.C., the date generally accepted, it would have taken place ten years *before* the census of Quirinius. Scholars say there was no Roman census under Herod's rule and one would not have been required anyway in Judea and Galilee, his territory. Whether Mary and Joseph were in Bethlehem for a census or to swear an oath, or for some other reason, Luke and Matthew's gospels agree that Mary gave birth there. In Matthew, the wise men find Mary and the Christ child in a house (Matthew 2:11) while Luke states that there was no room in the inn and so she gave birth to "her first newborn son, and wrapped him in swaddling clothes, and laid him in a manger" (Luke 2:7).

MORE THAN A STAR IN THE EAST Herod did not know about the star until the Three Wise Men, or Magi, arrived in Jerusalem and inquired about the birth of the King of the Jews. They mentioned that they had seen the star in the east and took it as a sign of an important birth of a king. Of the four New Testament gospels, only Matthew mentions the star, and apparently no one saw it but the wise men. But what did they see—a comet, an unusual alignment of planets, an eclipse, or something else?

The composition of a comet is ice and rock. It may have a super elongated orbit, and some comets may be visible for weeks or even months. It's possible that the wise men saw a comet. But ancient astrologers saw comets as a sign that an enthroned king would die or that a war might begin, so this would not have been an auspicious sign heralding a new king.

Other sources suggest the "star in the east" was more likely a conjunction of two planets passing close to each other. In early April, 6 B.C., and toward the end of the reign of Herod, Jupiter could be seen in the eastern sky in the astrological sign of Aries the Ram. The ancient Greeks and Romans believed that the most auspicious time for the emergence of a king was when Jupiter was in that position. Astronomer Michael R. Molnar asserts in his book, *Revealing the Star of Bethlehem: The Legacy of the Magi,* that the Moon was very near Jupiter, and the Sun, Jupiter, and Saturn were all in Aries. Aries was the sign of the Jews. These heavenly bodies then moved in such a way as to be seen as an important portent for the birth of a powerful future king of the Jews.

✂︎⚬✂︎

CONFLICTING STORIES OF THE VIRGIN BIRTH

Mark, the oldest of the four gospels of the New Testament and the one widely believed to have been the first written, does not record a virgin birth for Jesus. Neither does the Gospel of John. Scholars say that the later gospels of Matthew and Luke most likely drew upon Mark as source material. If that is true, then why did Matthew include the story of the virgin birth when it was not found in Mark?

Matthew states, "When as his mother Mary was espoused to Joseph, before they came together, she was found with child of the Holy Ghost" (Matthew 1:18). In other words, she had not been with a man but became pregnant through the power of the Holy Ghost.

Later, the Gospel of Matthew, considered by many to reflect the most Jewish tradition of the four gospels, makes the point that the virgin birth fulfilled Old Testament prophecy that a virgin would be with child and bring forth a son, "and they shall call his name Emmanuel, which being interpreted as 'God with us'" (Matthew 1:23). Matthew, by linking the virgin birth to Jewish tradition and prophecy, makes it clear that the son of Mary was the anticipated messiah, or savior of the Jews.

Where did Matthew get his information that Mary had become impregnated by the Holy Spirit if there were only two witnesses to the Annunciation, namely, the angel and Mary? The angel later revealed the mystery to Joseph, so perhaps Joseph told someone and the story spread and became part of an oral tradition that writer of the Gospel of Matthew heard. We'll probably never know the source for Matthew's information, but that gospel appears to emphasize Jesus' fulfillment of the prophecy of Isaiah 7:14, which states, "Therefore the Lord himself shall give you a sign: Behold, a virgin shall conceive, and bear a son, and shall call his name Immanuel."

The Gospel of Luke also proclaims a virgin birth. Luke states that "Mary kept all of these things, and pondered them in her heart" (Luke 2:19, 51). That suggests that she was not inclined to gossip about the miraculous events unfolding in her life. How could the writer know she kept those things inside and pondered them unless she revealed them to someone who passed the information through others to the writer of that gospel?

Some argue for the historicity of the virgin birth precisely because it is mentioned in two texts and independently of each other. Others say that of the four gospels, only Matthew and Luke alone wanted to have the birth of Jesus fulfill the Old Testament prophecy. Still others say that the early Christians may have borrowed from pagan traditions, in which gods impregnated women to produce divine sons. But that argument is flawed because the woman does not remain a virgin once the sexual act is initiated and, therefore, the conception is not virginal.

Here's a final note about the word "virgin." In Isaiah 7:14, "virgin" may be a Greek mistranslation of the original Hebrew word *almah,* which means "young woman." The Hebrew word for virgin is *bethulah*. However, a young woman who has never had intercourse is still a virgin.

❧❦❧

WHO WERE THOSE THREE WISE MEN? The Gospel of Matthew refers to the wise men in the plural, so there were two or more. Eastern tradition claims there were twelve. Early Christian fathers accepted three. Guided by the "star in the east" (also the "Star of Bethlehem"), they sought the place where Jesus was born to pay homage to him and to offer gifts. The Gospel of Matthew mentions the three gifts of the Magi: gold, an emblem of glory and divinity; frankincense, a symbol of purity and ascending prayer; and myrrh, a fragrant burial oil for the time of death.

The Magi (plural of magus, meaning sorcerer or shaman) may have been Zoroastrian priests from the East, perhaps from Persia or Babylon, where a remnant of the Hebrew population remained after Babylonian captivity. The Magi, often called the Three Kings, weren't really kings. More correctly, they might have been called "makers of kings."

Other sources identify the Magi as not only priests but astrologers whose job it was to keep an agricultural calendar and to advise nations and kings of portents and signs gleaned from what they observed in the sky. The ancient Hebrews considered astrology as divination and its practitioners as idolaters. Only Hebrew priests kept the calendar for religious purposes. Centuries after the birth of Christ, Marco Polo supposedly saw the graves of the Three Wise Men or Magi in what is today Tehran, Iran.

"Away In a Manger" Confusion

"AWAY IN A MANGER," ED. JAMES R. MURRAY (1841–1904)

Away in a manger, no crib for His bed,
The little Lord Jesus laid down His sweet head.
The stars in the sky looked down where He lay,
The little Lord Jesus asleep on the hay.

The cattle are lowing, the Baby awakes,
But little Lord Jesus, no crying He makes.
I love thee, Lord Jesus, look down from the sky.
And stay by my cradle till morning is nigh.

"Away in a Manger" is an American Christmas carol. The original song had two verses that were written by an anonymous author. The first two verses are believed to have been composed in approximately 1880. A third verse was added some time later.

James R. Murray was the composer who first published the work in a children's book of songs, titled *Dainty Songs for Little Lads and Lassies,* and in that collection called the song "Luther's Cradle Hymn," leading to confusion over the authorship. The song was often sung to the tune of "Luther's Cradle Hymn," a piece written by William J. Kirkpatrick, a Pennsylvanian who served in the Union army during the Civil War and composed a number of beautiful Christian hymns.

the history of christmas

*C*hristmas evolved out of the ancient world of miracles and magic. Many sources say that the early Christians did not celebrate the birthday of Jesus but did pay solemn homage to him at Easter. Early church theologian and scholar Origen (185–254) objected to the celebration of Jesus' birthday, apparently believing that birthday parties were not for the holy and virtuous. During ancient times, Christians in the East managed to celebrate Jesus' birthday along with his baptism during the annual Epiphany observances on January 6. Eventually, in the fourth century in Constantinople, a feast day was established to honor Jesus' birthday. If Christmas evolved from miracles and magic, then we all must wonder what is real. What is true? Let's take a look at the history of this splendid holiday.

WHY DECEMBER 25? Early Christian leaders who decided upon December as Jesus' birth month may have made a calculated choice based upon a belief that integrating pagan cultural traditions with Christianity might be a wise thing to do. In pagan cultures of that time, people enjoyed participating in winter solstice festivals. Christian leaders understood that forbidding people to participate in those popular cultural festivals might have the effect of turning them away from the faith. While some church fathers, such as Gregory Nazainzus, argued against any mixing of pagan practices with Christian ways, others believed such a conflation might be advantageous.

During ancient times, the winter solstice festival was celebrated according to the prevailing traditions of individual lands and regions. For example, the twelve-day Mesopotamian holiday known as Zagmuk, featured the symbolic sacrifice of the king. Since the people did not want to lose their king, a convict was sacrificed instead. His death expiated the sins of the people.

Wooden representations of the enemies of Marduk, the sun god, were torched, to symbolize Marduk's victory over disorder and darkness. This tradition may have established a precedent for the burning of the Yule log. Sacrifice was also an element of the midwinter Sacaea festival in Babylonia and Persia. That renewal festival featured a temporary subversion of roles. In other words, the slave became master and the master served his slave. During that holiday, two criminals were selected to receive sentences of either death or freedom. The one to be sacrificed was first jeered as a fake king. His death symbolized redemption for the sins of the people. The ritual had resonance in the death of Jesus and the freeing of Barabbas. Saturnalia, a Roman winter solstice festival that took place from December 17 to December 24, perhaps most closely resembles our modern Christmas celebration. During Saturnalia, children enjoyed a school break, people made and gave small gifts to family and friends, and everyone participated in celebratory meals. The social order of master and slave was reversed during Saturnalia. Although slaves could treat their masters anyway they wanted during the holiday period, they understood that the social order would inevitably revert back, so many undoubtedly used caution to guide their behavior. There was a special market established during Saturnalia and open gambling was allowed. Saturnalia was originally a one-day festival but grew to last a week. Celebrants honored Saturn, god of sowing. Roman festivals often included a public banquet and Saturnalia was no exception. Similar to the Zagmuk and Sacaea traditions, during Saturnalia, a person—perhaps a Roman banquet guest—was sacrificed. Wax candles known as cerei were burned to bring light and banish darkness. People dressed in colorful clothing and everyone wore the freedman's hat.

As Saturnalia ended and the calends of January or the first day of the New Year began, people were already socializing at parties. The calends was observed over the first three days of the month. During that period, homage to Strenia, originally known as Sabine, Roman goddess of the New Year, served as inspiration for people to walk from her sacred grove up the Capitoline Hill to present bay and palm branches and to offer gifts of dates, figs, or honey. These gifts were known as *strenae*. The word survives today in the French language as *etrennes* or New Year's gifts.

Many of the church's initial battles over what some Christians considered irreverent pagan practices associated with solstice festivities ended in a compromise. The Christmas tradition, consequently, absorbed some of those ancient pagan rites and symbols.

The actual day of the winter solstice is the twenty-four hour period extending from December 21 to December 22. So, why did the early Christians choose December 25 and not the actual date of the solstice? Some scholars suggest that the date had relevance and resonance with a prominent Hellenistic mystery religion during the Roman era that shared similarities with Christianity—Mithraism. Depending on which version of Mithra's birth story you read, he was born from either a rock, a tree, or a cosmic egg. The Mithraic faithful treated December 25, the birthday of their god, as a major holiday. Roman emperor Aurelian, a proponent of the cult of Sol, the sun-god, made "Sol Invictus" (Invincible Sun) the empire's pre-eminent diety in A.D. 354. Aurelian is believed to have established the holiday celebrated on December 25 known as *dies natalis Solis Invicti* (the birthday of the undefeated sun). Later, Constantine, who ruled a century after Aurelius and converted to Christianity during the final moments of his life, decreed a Roman day of rest (*dies solis*), meaning literally "day of the Sun" or Sunday. The themes of defeat of darkness, the restoration of light, and renewal of hope that were integral to Mithraism and other solstice traditions were easily adapted into early Christianity. Christ, in his death and resurrection, exemplified these very important elements. People simply shifted their devotion from the sun to the Son of God and thus Christianity supplanted the Roman pagan worship of the sun deity. December 25 became the day that marked Christ's birth. Christians, thanks to Constantine, could legally practice their faith, marking holy days such as Christmas with special festivities.

By the fifth century, the Western Roman Empire came under siege by barbaric invaders. Nordic and Germanic barbarians, often led by powerful warrior chiefs, launched assaults and penetrated into Roman border lands. Their marches, deeper into the Roman Empire, gave them exposure to Christian ideas and the celebration of Christmas. The conversion of these barbarians helped the spread of Christian ideas. The Celts and Germans in the lands north and west of the Empire already had ancient traditions celebrating the winter solstice. These were later integrated into the European Christmas holiday. An old Germanic festival known as Jul (from Julmond meaning "December") celebrated the triumph of life over death, renewal, and regeneration. An agricultural festival, Jul subsequently became "Yule." Food and drink items were made from wheat, widely recognized in some agricultural societies as a symbol of life. Boughs of evergreens were displayed. Yule logs were burned, and the holiday meal featured a deliciously prepared boar's head. Tradition holds that an Oxford student took a book about Aristotle into the woods where he suddenly was attacked by a wild boar. Shoving his book into the boar's throat, he killed the animal and took it back to the university. The book was salvaged and the animal roasted. An orange was stuffed into the mouth. To this day, Queen's College at Oxford keeps alive the Boar's Head Ceremony in a celebration that includes singing the traditional carol and presenting the orange to the lead singer. References to such traditions have been preserved in boar's head carols, wassail lyrics, holly carols, and other types of Christmas carols.

✖✖◉✖✖

THE DAWN OF CHRISTMAS IN EUROPE Christianity eventually spread through Europe, bringing with it celebratory traditions of holy days such as Christmas. On December 25, in 598, Saint Augustine, the first Archbishop of Canterbury, allegedly baptized no fewer than 10,000 Britons.

There is some debate whether or not King Arthur and his Knights of the Round Table were the first individuals to introduce Christmas to the people of England in A.D. 521. Others point out that it may have been Saint Augustine who brought the holiday to that land in the sixth century. Pope Gregory I sent word to Augustine to adapt the English Yule festival into Christmas festivities. In particular, Augustine was to emphasize the importance of those specific traditions that had Christian relevance. The plan was successful, and the English have been celebrating Christmas ever since.

In Germany, the Synod of Mainz in A.D. 813 made Christmas an official religious holiday. Christmas began to be celebrated in Norway in the middle of the next century under the leadership of King Hakon the Good. By the ninth-century, all of Europe joined in Christmas celebrations that included feasting, gift giving, tree decorating, and candle lighting. By then, other older traditions associated with solstice festivals at that time of the year were either incorporated into Christmas activities or simply abandoned.

Protestants and Roman Catholics today celebrate Christmas on December 25. However, elsewhere in the world, for example, in Europe and certain Latin American countries, Christian churches mark two mid-winter holidays—Christmas and Epiphany—on January 6. (Here's a side note: A small number of British believers observed the January 6 tradition until about 1950—not because of any connection with the rites of Eastern churches, but because some of their own observances followed the old Julian calendar rather than the current Gregorian.).

The celebration of Christmas continued to evolve through each passing century as older pagan elements were abandoned. Alfred the Great of Great Britain liked the idea of celebrating Christmas for twelve days. In fact, he forbade people to work between Christmas and Epiphany and even made it illegal. In A.D. 878, Alfred remained faithful to his law and refused to go to war during those twelve days. Some say his refusal to do so handed victory to the Danes over the British during the Battle of Chippenham.

✄━━◦━━✄

LET THE FESTIVITIES BEGIN Christmas extravagance perhaps achieved its apogee in the mid-eleventh century in England. People dressed extravagantly for church services, but not as one might think. They put on masks and costumes just as they might on Halloween. Parishioners lifted their voices in songs, not only singing carols but off-colored ditties.

The altar became another flat surface for revelers to use for rolling their dice. Medieval clergy added humor to their sermons along with a dash of ribbing pointed at the church's solemnity. However, the sense of sacred was not entirely replaced by gluttony, games, irreverence, and comedy. People still engaged in heart-felt caroling and performing in nativity plays. The king and his court tried to outdo each other in their ostentatious displays of excess. For Christmas in A.D. 1252, Henry III supposedly had 600 oxen killed and prepared for a single feast—and that was just the main course! The feast also included salmon pie and roasted peacock. Merchants and other higher-ups paid their respects to the king by giving him gifts and cash. There were guidelines for gift giving based on one's social position. The aforementioned Henry III once closed down merchants until they paid their proper dues, although in 1248 he seemed to regain a bit of his Christmas spirit when he established a custom of giving food to the needy for the holiday.

Looking Back

At Christmas I no more desire a rose
Than wish a snow in May's new-fangled mirth;
But like of each thing that in season grows.

—William Shakespeare, *Love's Labour's Lost*

Gambling was also a big part of the festivities around the court. Stories of the royalty using loaded dice to ensure against losing seem to capture the spirit of the age. But royal excess at Christmas surely reached it apogee in

1377. In that year, we are told, Richard II had a Christmas feast for over 10,000 people. Records do not indicate whether the 2,000 cooks employed at the feast enjoyed the holiday.

Richard II was no rival for Henry VIII when it came to excess. When Henry wanted something very badly, he got it. Henry VIII initiated the break from the Roman Catholic Church after divorcing Catherine of Aragon and being excommunicated by the pope. He then proclaimed himself Supreme Head of the Church of England. In that capacity, he not only seized assets of the Roman Catholic Church that were in England, but also took control over ecclesiastical observances, such as Christmas. During Henry's tenure as King of England, Christmas became a time of extravagant celebration marked by sumptuous feasts and many holiday plays and dances. Successive heirs to the throne, including Henry's daughter Elizabeth I and James I, continued the elaborate festivities.

❧⚬❧

SCROOGES AND THEIR ATTEMPTS TO OUTLAW CHRISTMAS With the Protestant Reformation, these objections gained the backing of an organized power. Beginning in 1517 with the posting of Luther's Ninety-Five Theses, the Reformation attacked religious feasts and saint's days, among other things, as corrupt practices. Christmas was outlawed in Scotland in 1583.

The Protestants and Puritans of England also condemned the gluttony, drinking, and partying associated with Christmas celebrations and argued for all pagan customs to be done away with. Most Protestants observed Christmas as a day of quiet reflection; the Puritans, however, did not observe it at all. Strict interpreters of the Scriptures, the Puritans pointed to the injunction to devote six days to work and one to rest. Unless Christmas happened to fall on the Sabbath, it was considered a workday.

By the middle of the seventeenth century, the holiday was under fire. The feelings of previously small pockets of objectors began to have Mass impact as the political situation in England became increasingly unstable. From 1642 to 1649, the country was engaged in civil war as a result of the power struggle between the Stuart kings and Parliament. Over this time England entered its Commonwealth period and was ruled by Oliver Cromwell and the Puritans. Christmas's enemies began taking the first steps toward defeating the holiday. The government issued official policies outlawing all religious festivals. Take a look at the written policy:

"Whereas some doubts have been raised whether the next Fast shall be celebrated because it falleth on the day which, heretofore, was usually called the Feast of the Nativity of our Saviour, the lords and commons do order and ordain that published notice be given, that the Fast appointed to be kept on the last Wednesday in every month, ought to be observed until it be otherwise ordered by both houses; and that this day particularly is to be kept with the same solemn humiliation because it may call to remembrance our sins and the sins of our forefathers, who have turned this Feast, pretending the memory of Christ, into an extreme forgetfulness of him, by giving liberty to carnal and sensual delights."

—1644 British proclamation outlawing public Christmas revelries

The Puritan era was marked by such laws, updated over the years to be even stricter. At first, such declarations caused a great deal of upheaval among the people, who were unprepared for such a step and objected to the idea to begin with. In the initial days of these ordinances, the people tried to disobey, and there was even some rioting. Gradually, however, the Puritans won out.

And so Christmas was now outlawed, as were those who celebrated it in any way. Carols were deemed illegal and churches were locked, even to clergy.

Technically, the Puritans objected to Christmas not as a Christian event but as an excessive festival with pagan roots; apparently they believed the only way to deal with such impious doings was to abolish the day and everything associated with it. They meant to banish this "wrong" not only from the country but also from the hearts of its subjects. And they came very close to succeeding—but then came the Restoration.

✄❦✄

HALLELUIAH! CHRISTMAS BANS ARE LIFTED

Christmas was legitimized again when the monarchy, led by Charles II, returned to power in Great Britain 1660. The holiday could be observed freely again, and people were happy. The popular sentiment of the time was expressed in this verse:

Now thanks to God for Charles' return,
Whose absence made old Christmas mourn;
For then we scarcely did it know,
Whether it Christmas were or no.

With the good will of the new leaders, and with the lifting of the formal bans instituted under the Puritans, Christmas seemed to be positioned for a comeback of epic proportions in England. But it was not to be.

❦ Looking Back ❦

England was merry England, when Old Christmas was brought his sports again.
'Twas Christmas broach'd the mightiest ale;
'Twas Christmas told the merriest tale;
A Christmas gambol oft could cheer
The poor man's heart through half the year.

—Sir Walter Scott

The holiday was, at the outset of the Restoration, a shadow of what it had been. The pagan excesses and riotous elements were not the only things lost to the Puritan purge; the Christmas spirit seemed to have simply left many hearts and minds.

Indeed, although the Puritans had lost control, much of their philosophy still carried a lot of weight, and many carried on as if they were still in power. Christmas may have been legal, but it was still opposed by some powerful members of the clergy. This left a good many parishioners in a bind, and it kept the holiday from making much of a public recovery from the latter part of the seventeenth century onward. The middle of the eighteenth brought still more obstacles.

Surprising as it may seem, as the years passed and the Puritan era became a more and more distant memory, the outlook for Christmas actually got worse, thanks to continuing resistance from some member of the clergy and a changing social climate. By the time the industrial revolution began, all thoughts seemingly turned toward work; everything took a back seat to the quest for money and progress. In this fast-paced atmosphere, it appeared, there was simply no room for holidays.

Charles Dickens's stinging literary indictments of mindless greed and soul-crushing poverty appear not only in *A Christmas Carol* but in much of the rest of his work as well. The numbing, inescapable want of most British workers and their families was one of the chief reasons people had a hard time finding much to celebrate during this period.

At the end of the day, common people didn't have much to celebrate with, and they didn't have much time, either. England had entered into the era of child labor, miserable working conditions, and endless workweeks. Not that things were all bad—some benevolent employers actually gave their workers half the day off for Christmas.

Festive Fact

In 1761, the Bank of England closed for forty-seven holidays over the course of a year; in 1834, it closed for only four. Employees during the mid-nineteenth century considered themselves lucky to get a half-day off for Christmas.

Throughout this period, however, there were small, quiet groups of people who kept the holiday alive in their hearts and homes. But Mass enjoyment of the holiday would not take place again until the Victorian Era.

∾⊙∾

GERMANS KEEP THE FLAME ALIVE While public celebration of Christmas faced both religious objections and adverse social conditions in England, the German people were enjoying a wonderful and expansive Christmas tradition that had been building up over the centuries. It is very likely that the American love affair with Christmas that began in the late nineteenth and early twentieth centuries, so influential in the way the whole world now views the holiday, would have never occurred if it had not been for the enthusiastic influence of Christmas-loving German immigrants.

The Germans have long espoused the idea of keeping the spirit of Christmas alive inside—in one's heart, mind, and spirit—and turning that feeling outward in Mass celebration. The German Christmas is a Christmas of trees, gingerbread houses, cookies, feasts, and carols; most of all, it is the Christmas of childhood wonder and joy.

The Christmas season in Germany is about the longest anywhere: a month and a half. Starting with Saint Andrew's Night on November 30, the country throws itself into a festive abandon that doesn't wind down until January 13, the Octave of Epiphany. Between those days, sixteen holidays are observed, and life is filled with both strict devotion to the Christ child and joyous merriment. The cities are brimming with *Christkindlmarkts*

(Christ Child Markets), fairs, parades, and carolers. The smell of gingerbread and other delicious treats is in the air, and Christmas trees are everywhere.

The German people have had an enormous part to play in shaping Christmas into the form we know and love today. It has been said that the Germans had such an abundance of Christmas spirit that they gave some of it to the rest of the world.

One of the beneficiaries of the German love of Christmas was Victorian England. Victoria assumed the throne in 1837 at the age of eighteen; three years later she married Prince Albert, who became Prince Consort. Prince Albert, being of German descent, brought with him to England many of the wonderful Christmas traditions of his homeland. Christmas soon became a special occasion for the royal family; their celebration of it emphasized the importance of family closeness and an appreciation of children and revived the idea of the holiday meal and holiday decorations. In 1841, Prince Albert introduced the first Christmas tree to Windsor Castle; he was largely responsible for the later popularity of Christmas trees in England. Since Victoria and her family enjoyed an astonishing popularity that verged at times on religious adoration, much of what they did was widely emulated. Newspapers and magazines such as *The Illustrated London News* provided a hungry audience with chronicles of the royals' daily activities. Anything seen in the castle, it seemed, was soon copied in homes throughout the country, providing the British Christmas with a much-needed boost.

WHY DOES *Santa* WEAR RED?

A True Translation?: "Christ Was Born on Christmas Day"

"CHRIST WAS BORN ON CHRISTMAS DAY," TRADITIONAL GERMAN SONG

Christ was born on Christmas Day,
Wreathe the holly, twine the bay;
Christus natus hodie [Christ this day is born];
The babe, the Son, the Holy One of Mary.

He is born to set us free,
He is born our Lord to be,
Ex Maria Virgine [Of the Virgin Mary],
The God, the Lord, by all adored forever.

Let the bright red berries glow,
Ev'rywhere in goodly show,
Christus natus hodie;
The Babe, the Son, the Holy One of Mary.

Christian folk, rejoice and sing,
'Tis the birthday of a King,
Ex Maria Virgine;
The God, the Lord, by all adored forever.

"Resonet in Laudibus" was the Finnish title of a fourteenth-century German Christmas song of joy that became known as "Christ Was Born on Christmas Day" after John Mason Neale, an English clergyman and author, translated the work into English. The song is also known as "Nunc Angelorum." Neale wrote fifteen volumes of hymns and translations during his lifetime.

part three

the victorian christmas

*T*he Victorians influenced Christmas greatly and helped to instill traditions that we carry on today. They lavishly decorated their trees with tin toys, fruits, tin whistles, nuts, sweet candies, handmade dolls, gingerbread men, sugar cookies, and ribbon, and they carefully attached hand-dipped candles for light. No Victorian tree was complete without the addition of a star.

Doors and mantels were draped in fresh greenery. The Victorians also made scented pomanders by sticking cloves into oranges, lemons, or limes and hanging them with ribbons. They hung apples onto their Christmas trees. They slipped greenery inside glass balls with a little mistletoe. These became known as "kissing balls" because the balls were hung over doorways and when a couple passed under them, they were obliged to, well, kiss.

The Victorians turned Christmas decorating into a high art with the addition of German glass ornaments, icicles, and an angel perched on top of the tree. In a nutshell, people who love a decorative and festive holiday owe a lot to the people of the Victorian era! Let's take a look at the lasting impressions of the Victorian era.

MORE THAN A PARTY? The Victorians adored parties, and Christmas provided the perfect occasion for dinners, teas, and balls. The rapid growth of factories during the industrial revolution meant more people had more purchasing power for factory-produced items that were more affordable and readily becoming available.

Victorian families used their earnings to make Christmas the most wonderful time of the year for their children and friends. Baskets in the foyers of Victorian homes quickly filled with calling cards decorated with seasonal images like those captured by Currier & Ives and Louis Prang. Parties were often intimate with plenty of food and drink. So rich and strong was the eggnog that the horse might have to guide the trap home without the help of its tipsy driver.

❧ Looking Back ❧

Victorian eggnog consisted of the beaten yolks of a dozen eggs, as much sugar as could be dissolved, one glass of aged whisky, one whole grated nutmeg, and three pints of whole milk with cream. They finished the drink by beating the egg whites until frothy and stirring them into the eggnog.

❧⊙❧

DEFINING FAMILY TOGETHERNESS During the Christmas season, the Victorians placed emphasis on their children, family togetherness, and the Christ child. They spent time with family and friends, giving gifts, eating, drinking, attending church, and celebrating the joy of the season and they did not forget the families of their working-class servants.

On the first workday after Christmas, it was customary for churches to open their alms boxes to the poor, in an attempt to give some cheer to those who could not afford a very merry Christmas. Out of this custom grew Boxing Day, on which service people and other workers would collect money or treats from their employers. As part of the Victorian celebration, people placed gifts of money into small boxes and on Boxing Day (the day after Christmas) gave them to those who had provided them with loyal service throughout the year.

VICTORIANS REVIVE WASSAILING The Victorians were obsessed with keeping tradition alive and are considered responsible for reviving medieval wassailing. In agricultural areas of Europe during the Middle Ages, farmers traveling from one farm to the next poured hot wassail (a mulled wine made of apples and spices) on the roots of trees while making a loud racket to drive away the evil spirits that had brought upon them frigid air and shortened days. The practice may have had its roots in pagan ritual. The Victorians revived wassailing as caroling, traveling from one house to the next where they sang Christmas carols, sharing the spirit of Christmas with others wherever they went. No doubt to warm themselves, they drank a fair amount of wassail or perhaps even something a wee bit stronger.

WHY DOES *Santa* WEAR RED?

CAROLING, CAROLING THROUGH THE YEARS

The fourteenth century also saw the beginning of widespread caroling. Carols had been used in Roman churches as early as the second century. In the Middle Ages, they were used in conjunction with Nativity plays to convey the Christmas story to those who could not read. By the sixteenth century, the mummers, a traveling band of costumed carousers somewhat like street actors, were out and about.

Fortunately for historians and carol lovers alike, a young man named Richard Hill kept a written record of, among other things, the popular British carols of the time. Spanning the years 1500 to 1536, Hill's diary was extremely valuable in helping to keep alive such secular carols as "The Boar's Head Carol."

❧ ◉ ❧

"CLASSIC" CHRISTMAS DINNER

The arrival of Christmas Eve in a Victorian home was celebrated with a midnight supper, often after church service. After all that caroling and good cheer, there were bound to be some hungry mouths to feed. The Victorian Christmas menu is doubtless the one most people envision when thinking of a "classic" Christmas dinner. Middle-class families north of London served roast beef, while Londoners and those in southern England typically cooked a goose or turkey. Queen Victoria reportedly dined on beef and the choicest part of a roasted royal swan. Roast goose and sage and onion dressing were considered de rigueur in a typical 1870s Victorian Christmas dinner. The perfect accompaniment was red cabbage braised with spices and sugar, Yorkshire pudding, plum pudding soaked in brandy, and a mincemeat pie. To aid in digestion, there were games like Shadow Buff, the Memory Game, Poker and Tongs, and the Minister's Cat; there was also the ubiquitous sprig of mistletoe.

Little tokens were often slipped inside the Christmas dinner plum pudding, before serving. Good fortune came to those who found a treasure while eating the pudding.

❧⟁❧

CHRISTMAS REBORN AND RESTORED Gradually, over the course of Victoria's reign, the tide turned. Christmas once more had an important place in English life.

The Victorian Christmas commanded a special spirit, full of kindness and charity. The idea of giving and of concern for others, particularly those less fortunate, became ingrained in the Victorian consciousness during the Christmas season. As Charles Dickens said, Christmas was "the only time I know of, in the long calendar of the year, when men and women seem by one consent to open their shut-up hearts freely."

Dickens himself had a large role in reviving the Christmas spirit in his countrymen. With the publication of *A Christmas Carol* in 1843, people were reminded of what the holiday truly meant, all that it could be, and could bring to their lives.

The Christmas card was created during the Victorian Era, and it enjoyed great popularity. So did carols, which got their biggest boost since they had become legal again under Charles II. There was now caroling in church, caroling in homes, and bands of carolers roaming the streets. Most of the images we have today of outdoor carolers are from these times.

The custom of giving gifts on Christmas Day did not come about until the last few decades of the century; before that, England adhered to the old Roman tradition of waiting until New Year's Day. When Christmas eventually became the day for gifts, it was England's turn to borrow from America, whose Santa Claus became the model for the English Father Christmas.

By the beginning of the twentieth century, Christmas was fully reestablished as a holiday, steeped again in tradition and spirit. The Victorians had helped to mold a Christmas tradition that would forever alter the way Christmas was celebrated in England and America.

How Good Was He?: "Good King Wenceslas"

"GOOD KING WENCESLAS," BY JOHN MASON NEALE (1818–1866)

Good King Wenceslas looked out
On the feast of Stephen,
When the snow lay all about,
Deep and crisp and even.
Brightly shone the moon that night,
Though the frost was cruel,
When a poor man came in sight,
Gath'ring winter fuel.

"Hither, page, and stand by me,
If though know'st it telling,
Yonder peasant, who is he?
Where and what his dwelling?"
"Sire, he lives a good league hence,
Underneath the mountains,
Right against the forest fence,
By Saint Agnes' foundation."

"Bring me flesh, and bring me wine,
Bring me pine logs hither
Thou and I shall see him dine,
When we bear them thither."
Page and monarch, forth they went,
Forth they went together;
Through the rude wind's wild lament
And the bitter weather.

"Sire the night is dark now,
And the wind grows stronger,
Fails my heart, I know not how;
I can go lo longer."
"Mark my footsteps, my good page,
Tread thou in them boldly;
Thou shalt find the winter's rage
Freeze thy blood less coldly."

In his master's steps he trod,
Where the snow lay dinted;
Heat was in the very sod
Which the Saint had printed.
Therefore Christian men, be sure,
Wealth or rank possessing.
Ye who now will bless the poor
Shall yourselves find blessing.

Reverend John Mason Neale composed lyrics to this popular carol sung each year. The carol contains no references the Nativity of Jesus. The song does, however, mention the Feast of Stephen, which occurs on December 26 (Boxing Day in some countries) and places an emphasis on Christian charity. The song takes the form of a dialogue about giving food to a poor family. The dialogue is between the monarch and his page. According to various sources, the music of the song dates back to Finland some 300 years before 1853 when Neale wrote it. Wenceslas lived in the tenth century. He was a Bohemian who practiced Catholicism and ascended to the throne when he was eighteen. But he was not liked because of his prosyletizing and was murdered by his brother Boleslaw. Wenceslas became a martyr. He is the patron saint of the Czech Republic, and his feast day is September 28.

joy to the world: christmas around the globe

*C*hristmas traditions around the world are as varied as the people celebrating the holiday. In some countries, festivities continue for twelve days while in others the focus is on three: Christmas Eve, Christmas Day, and Boxing Day. Many people the world over decorate holiday trees. In some cultures, stockings are hung and filled with presents or fruits and nuts, while in others, presents are tucked in shoes or put into little red bags. In the United States, children put out cookies and milk as a snack for Santa. The trend in modern Ireland calls for mince pies and a bottle of Guinness. Regardless of their differences, people celebrating Christmas, almost without exception, place the greatest importance upon the joy of giving, the nearness of family, and remembrance of the birthday of the baby Jesus. Let's take a closer look at how countries around the globe celebrate in their own unique ways.

EUROPEAN CHRISTMAS As a general rule, the Christmas season in Europe begins in early December and lasts through January 6. The celebration is marked by beautiful and expansive Nativity scenes, huge feasts, and the observance of Epiphany. Though each ethnic group on the continent has its unique customs and rituals, there are elements that unify the holiday for all within a given country.

France

For the French, the winter holiday (known as Noël) is especially important for children. The season is a time to bask in the innocence and wonder of youth, while remembering and honoring the Holy Child who started it all.

Noël, from an expression meaning "day of birth," begins for most French on December 6, Saint Nicholas's Day. Saint Nicholas's Day is celebrated most heartily in the provinces, particularly in Lorraine, as it is believed that the Virgin Mary gave Lorraine to Nicholas as a gift; he is their patron saint. He is also, of course, the patron saint of children; little ones leave out their shoes in hopes that Saint Nicholas will leave gifts of nuts and candy during his night visit. In Lorraine there is a procession honoring the saint in which the figures of three boys in salt barrels are carted through the streets. These figures stand as a reminder of one of the saint's more lurid miracles: bringing three murdered boys back to life.

In some provinces of France, Saint Nicholas or Père Noël can be seen walking in a long red robe with a basket of goodies on his back, accompanied by Père Fouettard (Father Whipper), who dresses in an ugly black robe and takes care of bad children.

The signs of the season begin to appear rapidly after Saint Nicholas's Day. Homes, streets, shopping malls, cafés, and shops are decorated with lights, colorful decorations, and the image of Père Noël. While not as popular as in America, *sapins* (trees) are sold in outdoor markets; most who take trees home pot them so they will last longer and may be replanted later. The tree is decorated with glass, paper, or crocheted ornaments; a star, angel, or Père Noël is placed on top. While most French families use electric lights, some still use candles.

More important than a tree to the French home is the crèches, which are meant to look as realistic and beautiful as possible. To contribute to the realism, the children of Provence collect moss, pine, and rocks for the background. Some crèches contain *santons* (little saints) representing people in the Nativity. Santons came to France in the 1800s from Italy by way of Italian merchants; the figures are made of clay and in most cases are clothed with fabric.

The French crèche often depicts a French rather than Judean landscape. This could simply be a case of strong local influence on religious imagery, or it could have something to do with an obscure tradition hearkening back to the time when some areas of France claimed to be the birthplace of Christ. The regions of Provence, Auvergne, and Brittany have all made this claim in past eras. The climate and geography of these areas are considered to be similar to that of the Holy Land, and this coincidence may have something to do with the old claims.

Along with decorating, the preparations for the *reveillon* (awakening) must be completed by Christmas Eve day. Reveillon is the grand Christmas Eve feast that takes place after midnight Mass. The feast may have as many as fifteen courses, ranging from soups, fruits, salads, meats, fish, and chicken to cheese, breads, nuts, pastry, candy—all with plenty of wine. (This is, after all, France.)

The arrival of Christmas Eve sees the infant Jesus finally taking his place in the family crèche after a small family ceremony. Little children are put to bed to dream of the gifts that Père Noël may bring them. Previously, Petit Jesus, or Little Jesus, was the one who came to children on Christmas Eve. Later, the visitor was the spirit of Christmas, Père Noël. In present-day France, most children believe Jesus sends Père Noël in his place.

Unlike the American Santa, Père Noël is tall, dresses in a long red robe, and travels with a sack and a donkey. Though Père Noël is not seen in department stores as often as Santa is in the United States, he too can be contacted through a letter sent to the North Pole.

After the children are in bed, the older members of the family head off to midnight Mass. Along the way there are often processions reenacting the Nativity, some of which end in living crèches (where people play out the manger scene). The midnight Mass itself is very important in France, and almost everyone attends. At the Mass's conclusion, all head home to begin the reveillon.

❧ *Looking Back* ❧
The French feast following Christmas Eve midnight Mass often extends until dawn.

The reveillon often lasts the entire night, with no time for the adults to sleep before the children wander down to open their gifts. The adults wait until New Year's Day to exchange their gifts; some villages near the Spanish border mix Spanish and French traditions and open gifts on January 6.

The remainder of the vacation time surrounding this holiday is often spent either skiing in the French Alps or visiting the Riviera.

Belgium

Saint Nicholas arrives in Belgium on December 4 to take a look around and gauge children's behavior. On December 6 he delivers special treats to good children—and switches to bad ones. The children leave out hay and water for his horse or donkey along with their shoes as an added measure of goodness.

An area of the country known as Flanders is famous for its Nativity plays, which are performed with great care and attention to tradition. Three men who are chosen for their good behavior during the year dress as Magi and walk through the town. They sing songs at each house and are rewarded with snacks.

Everywhere in Belgium there are extensive processions on Christmas Eve. Each procession winds through the town, picking up members as it flows, until it reaches the church for midnight Mass.

Italy

Italy is the birthplace of the manger scene, or *presepio*, and it rightfully holds a place of distinction in the Italian Christmas. The *presepio* is filled with clay figures called *pastori* (the small saints the French call *santons*). All who come to the home kneel to pray or sing before the *presepio*.

In the days before Christmas, children visit homes and read Christmas selections, receiving a monetary reward. Over the twenty-four hours prior to Christmas Eve, a strict fast is observed, followed by a great meal. A unique feature of this evening is the Urn of Fate, a bowl filled with both presents and empty boxes. Each person picks to see whether he or she is "fated" to receive a gift—although no one ever really goes away empty handed.

Italian children receive gifts twice during this season. The Christ child is said to bring small gifts on Christmas Eve, but the more anticipated gift giving is from La Befana, who comes down the chimney on Epiphany Eve to leave goodies in shoes. Legend has it that La Befana was the woman who declined the Wise Men's offer to accompany them on their journey to see the Christ child. Regretting her decision later, she set out to bring the child gifts, but, as she never found him, she leaves gifts for other children instead. (The tradition has variants in many other countries, as well.)

Throughout the season, houses, stores, and streets are decorated in traditional ways, and there is much music and singing. The *ceppo* is an Italian version of the Christmas tree. Made of wood, the *ceppo* has the appearance of a ladder, with shelves linking two sides. The bottom shelf always contains a *presepio*; other shelves contain gifts and decorations.

As part of an older tradition, shepherds (*pifferai*) often come in from neighboring villages to play their horns and bagpipes before holy shrines and carpenter's shops, in honor of Joseph. In a role similar to that of the American Santa Claus, women dressed as La Befana collect for charities.

Christmas morning is occupied with the church Mass. As they have done for hundreds of years, Italian churches compete to see who has the most beautiful *presepio*. Popular opinion generally assigns that honor to the *presepio* of the Ara Coeli Church in Rome.

Spain

The Christmas season in Spain begins on December 8 with the Feast of the Immaculate Conception. An interesting feature of this feast is known as Los Seises, the Dance of Six, a custom in Seville in which boys perform a dance around the altar that symbolizes Christ's birth. Although the dance is still known by its original name, it is now performed by ten boys.

It is no surprise that the manger scene, or *nacimiento,* has a place of reverence in the Spanish Christmas. This manger scene contains all the traditional elements, with a few distinctly Spanish ones thrown in. Among the animals watching over Christ are a mule and *buey* (ox) and a stream of water is always included. Sometimes bullfighters are part of the on-looking crowd. These scenes are set up in public squares and in homes, taking precedence over Christmas trees, which are not common.

❧ Festive Fact ❧
The Spanish refer to Christmas Eve as Noche Buena (Good Night).

On Christmas Eve, family members gather in the room containing the nacimiento to sing hymns and pray. Late in the evening, the Misa de Gallo (Mass of the Rooster) is attended. Many Hispanic countries refer to midnight Mass as the Mass of the Rooster; it has been said that the only time a rooster ever crowed at midnight was the moment when Christ was born. After Mass, a big meal is often consumed.

Adults exchange gifts on Christmas Day. Another treat is the Spanish version of the Urn of Fate, in this case, a bowl filled with the names of everyone present. Two names are picked out at once; those whose names are chosen together are supposed to enjoy a lasting friendship or romance.

There is much dancing and other festivities through Epiphany, the day that children receive presents in their shoes from the Three Wise Men. (There is no Santa Claus figure.) Sometimes three men dress as the Magi and wander the streets singing before visiting the public *nacimiento*.

England

While the great traditions of the Yule log and boar's head are no longer commonly observed in England, in the minds of many they are an integral feature of the old-fashioned British Christmas. Dyed-in-the-wool traditionalists may substitute roast pig for the boar's head, but the modern fireplace is far too small to accommodate the massive Yule logs of times past. Even the great British roast beef has been replaced by turkey. Mince pie and plum pudding are still favorites, however, and the land that gave us the Christmas card is still sending them by the millions.

In England, the Christmas tree has been widespread since Prince Albert introduced the custom in 1841. Caroling and bell ringing are very popular, as well. Father Christmas, very similar to the American Santa Claus, leaves gifts for children. Letters to him are not mailed, but rather thrown in the fire; if they fly up the chimney, the desired gift is considered as good as brought.

Children hang up their stockings on Christmas Eve. After the children are in bed, parents decorate the tree and fill the house with holly, ivy, and mistletoe. Afterward, many go to a midnight Christmas service. In the morning children open gifts, and all sit down to that turkey dinner in the afternoon.

An additional observance at this time of year is Boxing Day, held on December 26. The name is taken from the old custom of opening the alms boxes in church the day after Christmas to give money to the needy.

Wales

Carol singing in Wales has become an art form. Nowhere in the world are Christmas carols more carefully crafted and lovingly sung. Each village has a trained choir and great gatherings for group singing.

The Christmas season is also the time for the Mari Llwd to appear. This odd creature is represented by a man wearing a sheet and carrying a horse's skull (or wearing a fake horse's head). The "creature" dances around in public and tries to bite people with the horse's jaws. If he manages to bite you, you must give him money!

The Christmas service is called Plygain and goes from 4:00 A.M. until sunrise on Christmas morn. Pulling taffy is one way to spend the day; in Wales, taffy is as much a part of Christmas fare as candy canes are in America.

Ireland

Christmas in Ireland is more religious and less festive than in other parts of Europe. Lit candles are left in the windows on Christmas Eve to light the Holy Family's way, but there are seldom many other decorations. The door to the home is left open on Christmas Eve so that the Holy Family may partake of the bread and milk left out on the table. Father Christmas is the gift giver here, and some presents are given out.

✤ Festive Fact ✤

In Great Britain, on the day after Christmas some engage in "hunting the wren." This old tradition called for the killing of a wren to symbolize the death of the old year. The dead wren was put on a stick so the hunters could parade it from house to house, singing carols. The homeowner would give the hunters some small tokens, and they would give him or her a feather for good luck.

Scotland

Christmas was not celebrated in Scotland until the 1960s; the once-out-lawed holiday was long seen as just another workday. Things have gradually changed, but to the Scots, Christmas is still not the major event that it is to many other peoples. New Year's Day is still the more important celebration.

Germany

Perhaps more than any other country, Germany has influenced the way Christmas is celebrated around the world. It is from Germany that we get some of the most popular ideas associated with the Christmas season and the Christmas spirit, as well as such welcome innovations as the Christmas cookie.

Things get started on Saint Nicholas's Day (December 6). Advent wreaths and calendars make their appearance, and this day marks the beginning of the German Christmas season.

It is said that the tradition of the Christmas tree began in Germany, and most modern families there would consider it unthinkable to pass the holiday without a tree. The tree is usually trimmed by the mother, who decorates with balls, tinsel, stars, cookies, marzipan, and so on. No one else is allowed to see the tree until Christmas Eve.

After Mass or church on Christmas Eve, the Christkind or Kris Kringle—not Saint Nicholas—brings the gifts. At first, the Christkind was meant to be the Baby Jesus; later the name came to stand for a more angelic figure that embodies the spirit of the Christ child. The Christkind wears a flowing white robe, a white veil, and gold wings. He often enters by an open window and rings a bell when gifts have been left. The name later evolved into Kris Kringle; it is in no way a pseudonym for Santa Claus. Like Saint Nicholas, Kris Kringle is accompanied by a nasty companion called Knecht Rupprecht, Pelznickle, or Ru-Klas.

Austria

Saint Nicholas's Day opens the Christmas season in Austria. Called SanterKlausen, the saint arrives not with a nasty helper for the holidays, but with the devil himself! (This is an extreme but not uncommon variation on the "dark companion" theme.) Both figures test the children, and the good ones get presents.

In Austria, the Nativity scene is displayed around the family tree, which is decorated with cookies as well as ornaments. There are processions known as "Showing the Christ Child." Nativity plays are also performed; similar to the Mexican *posadas*.

On Christmas Eve, many enjoy music from the *Turmblasen,* a brass band that plays carols from church steeples or towers. Later there is midnight Mass.

Both December 25 and 26 are legal holidays. The days are spent relaxing, socializing, and feasting on carp, ham, goose, pastry, and the like.

One of Austria's most important contributions to the celebration of Christmas is a song sung by church choirs and carolers around the world: "Silent Night." On Christmas Eve, 1818, organist Franz Gruber composed the music to accompany Josef Mohr's poem. The carol was Gruber's only published musical work. Today, it is certainly hard to imagine Christmas without that song.

Switzerland

As Switzerland is populated by four distinct groups of people, it has no dominant holiday tradition. Those with French backgrounds follow French customs; Germans, Italians, and Romansh speakers likewise follow their own traditions. Regardless of nationality, however, all in Switzerland celebrate with mangers and trees.

🎄 Festive Fact 🎄
Switzerland (a nation with four official languages) has multiple Christmas traditions, with no single approach to observing the holiday.

In some parts of Switzerland, great care is taken to emphasize the holiday's religious significance before its festive side. Children are not allowed to open their gifts until all have gathered around the tree to sing songs and read the story of the Nativity from the Bible. Presents are brought by the *Chriskindli*; the angelic figure arrives in town on a sleigh loaded with goodies and pulled by six reindeer.

Churches in Switzerland are famous for their bells, and bell-ringing competitions are held in some areas, such as Valais, on Christmas Eve. Saint Stephen's Day, December 26, has become an extension of the Christmas celebration in Switzerland.

Russia

Perhaps the best way to look at the Russian Christmas is to go back to the customs of pre-Revolutionary Russia, when Christianity flourished. Father Frost was a staple of the old tradition, and presents were brought by Babushka, Russia's version of the old woman who was supposed to have declined to join the Wise Men. There was also a girl dressed in white called Kolyada who would visit houses, singing carols and giving treats. Christmas trees were decorated.

Members of the Russian Orthodox Church would fast until after church services on Christmas Eve. Some communities engaged in the Blessing of the Water; sometimes a priest would go through the village with this water to bless the houses.

In the years following the revolution, many of the customs of Christmas were hard to track down, as they were for all intents and purposes illegal—or at least counter to the official pronouncements of the Party. Now that the Communist regime has passed, it is a good bet that many of those traditions will come back into prominence.

<div align="center">~~~◦~~~</div>

CELEBRATIONS IN CENTRAL AMERICA, THE WEST INDIES, AND THE CARIBBEAN

Christmas in Central America and the West Indies is characterized not by snow and sleigh bells but warm weather and bright flowers. For the most part, the countries in this area adhere to the traditions of the midnight Mass and Nativity scenes. On Christmas Eve there are often processions with people wearing costumes and carrying the manger; large festive meals are eaten on either Christmas Eve or Christmas Day. On Christmas Day there are picnics, bullfights, and other good times. A small number of Christmas trees are imported from the United States, and Santa is seen on occasion, but not to bring gifts. Gifts are put in children's shoes on January 6th by the Three Kings or the Christ child. These are the common aspects of the holiday; there are also a number of customs unique to individual countries.

Mexico

The Christmas season in Mexico begins on December 16, the first day of *posadas*. *Posada* is the Mexican word for a tradition popular among many Hispanic countries, the commemoration of the Holy Family's pilgrimage. *Posadas* take place over a period of nine days before Christmas; in each *posada,* the faithful act out Mary and Joseph's search for lodging. People travel to one another's homes, taking on the roles of holy pilgrims or nasty innkeepers.

The ritual culminates in celebration and prayer around the family altar, on which is placed a crèche and a covering of pine branches and moss. The houses are decorated with Spanish moss, evergreens, and paper lanterns. Also present are "The Flowers of the Holy Night," or poinsettias. After the religious portion of the *posada* is over, there is much merriment, with food, fireworks, and piñatas. The final and most important *posada* takes place on Christmas Eve. The Baby Jesus is placed in the cradle amid prayer and song. Afterward, everyone attends midnight Mass.

For Catholics the festivities end here. Christmas Day is quiet, and there is no Santa Claus figure. Children receive their gifts on Epiphany. For Protestants, however, the *posadas* are a bit different. There is more outdoor caroling, and children receive a gift bag from Santa during a church service early on Christmas Eve.

Honduras

Hondurans have their own version of *posadas*. For nine days before Christmas, the faithful act out Mary and Joseph's search for lodging. One house in the village is chosen to be the place of shelter, where people go to sing and pray. As there are many poor, the missions are important in providing holiday festivities for children. Tamales are served, dances and fireworks displays are held, and people visit each other's crèches.

Costa Rica

In Costa Rica, the Nativity scene is given its own room, not just a spot in a corner or on a table. In accordance with the climate, the decorations consist of brilliantly colored flowers and wreaths of cypress leaves and red coffee berries. Children put out their shoes for the Christ child to fill, as their parents did, but Santa is beginning to show up more and more.

Nicaragua

By late November, festivities have started in Nicaragua. Children gather in the streets with bouquets to honor the Virgin Mary with song. This portion of the holiday ends on December 8, with the Feast of the Immaculate Conception. On December 16, the Novena to the Holy Child begins; another kind of *posada,* it concludes on Christmas Eve at midnight Mass.

Panama

Schoolchildren in Panama engage in pre-Christmas activities much like the ones enjoyed by American children. Decorations and cards are made, gifts are exchanged, and there are plays. Requests for gifts are sent to Baby Jesus in Heaven, however, not to Santa Claus.

Puerto Rico

Understandably, there is a large American influence on the Puerto Rican Christmas, which features a mixture of Spanish and American traditions. Puerto Ricans have Santa Claus and a tree, but they receive gifts on both Christmas and Epiphany. Before Christmas there is a great deal of neighborhood caroling, with people dressing up as they believe the Magi did. Nine days before Christmas, a kind of *posada* begins in the form of the Mass of the Cards, which is held every day at 5:30 A.M.

A fun Christmas Eve tradition is Asalto, in which a band of people appears on someone's lawn to shout, sing carols, and plead for goodies. The owner usually opens up his or her house to them; after a small party, the group moves on to another house.

Dominican Republic

On the hot Caribbean island of the Dominican Republic, Christmas is celebrated not with a visit from Santa Claus but rather the three kings named Melchior, Gaspar, and Balthasar. One tradition asserts that Balthasar was king of Arabia, Melchior was king of Persia, and Gaspar was king of India.

Each family adorns their tree with special decorations, topping it with an angel or a star to represent the "star of the East" or "star of Bethlehem." The faithful attend a midnight Mass on Christmas Eve and also on Christmas morning. Traditional Dominican food is served for the feast on Christmas Eve, often featuring turkey (a rare treat) or pork. Mints are left for the Three Kings, and gifts are given to the children. The holiday formerly was celebrated on the eve of January 5, the night before Epiphany, but people eventually came to prefer December 25 as the day to celebrate Christmas. The children like it better, too, because it gives them more time (over their school break) to play with their gifts.

Brazil

Brazil is one South American country that has incorporated some American ideas for Christmas. Brazilians have a Santa equivalent called Papa Noël, lighted Christmas trees, and similar gift giving traditions. The manger, or *pesebre*, is still very important, however. On Christmas Eve a meal is laid out before the household attends midnight Mass, so that the Holy Family may eat if they wish. Children put out shoes for Papa Noël to fill. Because of the warm climate, Christmas Day is often filled with picnics and sport.

~~~∾◦∾~~~

"DO THEY KNOW IT'S CHRISTMASTIME AT ALL?" In most African countries, Christians make up only a small part of the population, so Christmas is usually not celebrated on a grand scale.

Although Christmas has been a tradition in Ethiopia for quite some time, observance in most other countries is limited to areas with established missions. In these areas Christmas is observed simply, in a way that many feel reflects the true meaning of the day. The missions provide homes and schools for the young children and hospitals for the ill; at Christmastime, the efforts of all are concentrated on helping those in need and on the spiritual aspects of the holiday. There are no Santas or trees, and there is very little gift giving, except to the poor. In some places, lucky children receive sugar, grains, or fruit.

In Algiers there are a number of Catholic churches that celebrate midnight Mass. Streets are colorfully decorated.

The Christian church in Ethiopia is the Coptic Church. Believers there still abide by an older calendar, which places Christmas on January 7.

Things stray from the norm a bit in Ghana. There, Christmas evergreen or palm trees are seen, but only in churches, and there is a Father Christmas who comes out of the jungle. Children have school pageants, and there is more gift giving. Early Christmas morning, a group enacts the story of the shepherds and angels heralding Christ's birth, traveling the streets and singing songs.

❧ Festive Fact ❧

Christmas is a low-key affair in Africa; its observance is usually limited to relatively small Christian populations. The emphasis is typically on charitable acts and simple presents.

It's fair to say that in most African countries, Christmas could be ignored entirely without changing the cultural landscape much. One exception to this, however, is found in South Africa. Christmas there falls in the midst of summer vacation, so the activities are adapted to the warmer weather. In the European sections of the country, shops are decorated and streets are lit. Father Christmas puts gifts in the children's stockings. After a church service on Christmas Day, the Christmas feast is eaten outside.

⌒◦⌒

A VISIT TO BETHLEHEM Each year, thousands of Christians make the pilgrimage to Bethlehem for what is perhaps the most moving Christmas celebration of them all. This is true even though Muslims and Jews make up most of the population of the Middle East.

WHY DOES *Santa* WEAR RED?

Christians come to visit the place where, according to the gospels, it all began. Not surprisingly, this is the time of the year when Bethlehem is most popular. The festivities in the "little town" center on the Church of the Nativity and the Shepherds' Fields. The Church of the Nativity is believed to stand on the place where Christ was born; under the church, within a small cave, a star on the floor marks the place where Mary gave birth to Jesus. The Shepherds' Fields is said to represent the fields where the angels announced the arrival of Christ.

Among the indigenous Christians in Bethlehem, there are three groups. The Roman Catholics celebrate Christmas on December 25, the Greek Orthodox on January 6, and the Armenian Christians on January 18. Representatives protecting the interests of these three groups sit on a board that "governs" the Church of the Nativity, so that no group is favored or slighted. Services are not held within the church itself but rather in an adjoining building. Services on Christmas Eve are by invitation only, but they are televised to the crowds outside. Afterward, most venture to the Shepherds' Fields, which are also divided into three sections.

With the obvious exception of Israel, the peoples of the Middle East are predominantly Muslim. Some of these Muslim countries do have Christian sections, and in those sections Christmas is observed, although the observance is usually more strictly religious, as in Africa. Some countries, however, have indigenous Christian populations that have been celebrating Christmas for centuries.

Armenia

It is believed that Christmas should be celebrated on the day of Christ's baptism, which is January 6 in most church calendars. However, the Armenian Church follows the old Julian calendar, which marks this date as January 19. One week before Christmas there is a fast, during which no meat, eggs, cheese, or milk may be eaten. Religious services are held on Christmas Eve and Christmas Day. Afterward, children go onto the roofs with handkerchiefs and sing carols; the handkerchiefs are often later filled with fruit, grain, or money.

Iraq

In the reputed home of the Magi, Christmas is known as the Little Feast (Easter being the Great Feast). Christians here fast from December 1 until Christmas Eve, consuming no meat, eggs, milk, or cheese. After the evening church service, a great feast begins, but there is no gift exchange.

Syria

Syrian Christians celebrate Christmas longer than most Middle Eastern countries, beginning on December 4, Saint Barbara's Day, and lasting through Epiphany, January 6. Children receive gifts on Epiphany from the Camel of Jesus. Syrian children believe that an animal brings their gifts. Tradition holds that the youngest of the Wise Men's camels was so exhausted from the long journey that it fell next to Jesus' manger. There, the Christ child blessed the little camel and it became known as the Camel of Jesus.

A tradition left over from the days of religious persecution is the locking of the outside gate of the house on Christmas Eve. This is to remind all that they once had to practice their religion behind closed doors. The father lights a great fire in the courtyard, and the youngest son reads from the Gospel. The way the fire burns is said to predict the family's fortune for the upcoming year. Hymns are sung. After the fire has been reduced to embers, family members make a wish and jump over them.

Epiphany Eve is known in Syria as Lilat-al-Kadr (Night of Destiny). A magic mule brings presents to children on this night. The mule's magic powers derive from when he was caught up as the trees bowed at midnight on the night of Christ's birth.

Surrounding countries of Syria celebrate Christmas in their own way, too. In Pakistan, many aspects of the Christmas celebration are similar to those in America. There's even a Santa Claus!

In neighboring India, the Christmas trees are either banana or mango. Small oil-burning lamps serve as decorations. Many churches are made festive with the addition of red poinsettias. Indian Christians attend a midnight Mass on Christmas Eve. The custom in South India is for Christians to set out small clay lamps on the flat rooftops of their houses or in niches in the walls.

<hr />

FAR-EASTERN FESTIVITIES In the Far East there are perhaps fewer Christians than there are in the Middle East. As in Africa, the existence of a Christian population there is largely due to missionary work.

China

China was only opened to the West 400 years ago, so relatively speaking, Christians and Christmas have not been around for long. A minute portion of the Christian population celebrates a Christmas heavily influenced by the missionaries. Christmas is referred to as Sheng Dan Jieh, or the Holy Birth Festival. There are trees, called "trees of light," and paper lanterns are intermingled with holly for decoration. Stockings are hung, and there is a version of Santa known as Lam Khoong-Khoong (nice old father), or Dun Che Lao Ren (Christmas old man). Gift giving has some formal rules. Jewelry and other more valuable gifts are given to the immediate family; other gifts are given to relatives and friends.

More important to the majority of Chinese is the New Year, referred to as the Spring Festival, which is celebrated in late January. New toys and clothes are given, and feasts are held. The spiritual aspects concern ancestor worship, and portraits of ancestors are displayed on New Year's Eve. This is not strictly speaking a Christmas celebration, but it is a festive and popular seasonal undertaking.

Japan

Japan has roughly the same proportion of Christians to non-Christians as China. Christmas there is celebrated by a large number of people—including a good many that follow other religions. For the Japanese, Christmas is a strictly secular celebration, considered a time for fun and gifts. There are Japanese versions of American Christmas carols; department stores have Christmas trees and Christmas sales; holly, bells, and decorations are everywhere. Some believe that the Japanese awareness of Christmas is due in part to their large manufacturing interests in America.

The religious aspects of the Japanese Christmas are confined to the areas touched by missionary work. In those parts, Christmas is celebrated with services, hymns, children's pageants, visits to hospitals, and other services for the needy.

Korea

Typical for this part of the world, Korea has a small pocket of Christians who celebrate Christmas with traditional religious services. Schoolchildren put on pageants, and there is a great effort put into helping the needy. For the actual Christmas service, a group of adults and children stay awake in the church on Christmas Eve. At around 2 A.M., they go out into the neighborhood singing, and they are often invited into homes for a treat. Religious services are held in the morning, and there is much caroling as people make their way there.

For the country as a whole, Christmas is a holiday, although the majority of the population is Buddhist. Some families have trees, and children are given small gifts.

❧◦❧

CHRISTMAS CELEBRATIONS FAR AND NEAR Wherever they are, people are celebrating Christmas in their own way!

Canada

Christmas is celebrated in many different ways in Canada. The country is made up of a variety of ethnic groups, most of which celebrate Christmas in accordance with their own traditions.

Vancouver, on the western end of Canada, is illuminated with lights, especially in the harbor area, and trees are lit in homes. In Montreal, Masses are celebrated in the many beautiful cathedrals, and in Nova Scotia old carols are sung at home and in church. In Newfoundland, the inhabitants' fishing skills are put to work for the church. During Christmas week the daily catch is given to the church so that it can be sold to raise money for the church's work.

Australia

As in South Africa, Christmas "down under" falls during summer vacation. Because of the climate, flowers are the most important Christmas decoration, particularly the Christmas bush and the Christmas bell. Father Christmas and Santa exist side by side—like siblings, which they certainly are. Gifts are exchanged on Christmas morning before attending church. Typically, the afternoon is spent at the beach or engaging in sports.

Australia is also the home of "Carols by Candlelight," a tradition started by radio announcer Norman Banks in 1937. After Banks saw a woman listening to carols alone by candlelight, he decided to do something to relieve the loneliness and isolation some feel during the holidays. He announced a community carol-sing for anyone who wanted to join in. The concept has grown in popularity over the years, and the recorded program is now broadcast the world over.

"Joy to the World": Psalm to Hymn to Song!

"Joy to the World," by Isaac Watts (1674–1748)

Joy to the world! the Lord is come;
Let earth receive her King;
Let ev'ry heart prepare Him room,
And heav'n and nature sing,
And heav'n and nature sing,
And heav'n, and heav'n and nature sing.

Joy to the world! the Saviour reigns;
Let men their songs employ;
While fields and floods, rocks, hills, and plains
Repeat the sounding joy,
Repeat the sounding joy,
Repeat, repeat the sounding joy.

He rules the world with truth and grace,
And makes the nations prove
The glories of His righteousness,
And wonders of His love,
And wonders of His love,
And wonders, and wonders of His love.

"Joy to the World" combines the music of George Frederick Handel and the words of Englishman Isaac Watts, a prolific psalmnist and hymnist who produced some 600 hymns during his lifetime. He wrote "Joy to the World" in 1719. Watts apparently drew inspiration from Psalm 98 for the words to his carol; however, some people in his world did not appreciate his reworking of the psalm into a hymn. Putting the hymn to music from Handel's *Messiah* was the genius of Dr. Lowell Mason. Although "Joy to the World" was also put with other music, Mason's version became more popular and is the version we know today.

WHY DOES *Santa* WEAR RED?

santa: a man of myth, reality, and mispronounciation

*W*ho is the man who bellows "Ho, ho, ho"? The modern-day Santa we all know and love is an engaging combination of myth, reality, and mis-pronunciation. What follows is a brief account of the great man's evolution through the years. Let's take a detailed look at how Santa came to be the celebrity that he is and the man whom we all love!

THE LEGEND Beyond evidence that Nicholas was a very good man, there are the rumors and legends that suggest he was nothing short of otherworldly. His birth is said to have been a miraculous one, as his parents, according to legend, had been married thirty years and had long since given up hope of ever conceiving a child. And then, it is said that shortly after his birth he was able to stand up in his crib, as if praying.

Nicholas appears to have had no doubt about his vocation; he prepared to enter the monastery at a young age. Before devoting his life to his faith, however, he was required to rid himself of all his worldly possessions. The way in which he is said to have accomplished this has helped to establish his identification as a gift-giver.

As the story goes, there was a family in town with three daughters of marriageable age, but they were so poor that they had no dowry; no dowry meant no marriage. Nicholas, hearing of their plight, disguised himself and went at night to their house, where he threw three bags of gold coins down their chimney, saving the daughters from a life of prostitution. The gold is said to have landed in the girls' stockings, which were hanging in the fireplace to dry.

❧ *Looking Back* ❧
The tradition of stuffing gifts in Christmas stockings is probably rooted in a gift of gold coins attributed to Saint Nicholas.

As legend has it, the father of the family caught Nicholas in the act, and though Nicholas tried to swear him to secrecy, the story spread through the town quickly.

Shortly after entering the monastery, Nicholas became the Bishop of Myra. The church in Myra had been having great trouble replacing the former bishop, and the people were at their wits' end as to how to solve the dilemma. One night it came to a church official in a dream that the first one to enter the church for Mass the next day should be the new bishop; his name would be Nicholas. It happened that Nicholas had been traveling on a ship that encountered rough weather. He prayed for safety, and when he arrived on land he headed immediately for the church in Myra to give thanks; the rest is history.

During his lifetime, Saint Nicholas would undergo another rough voyage on a ship, a journey that would result in his being named patron saint of sailors. While returning from a pilgrimage to the Holy Land, the vessel that carried him ran into a terrible storm. Nicholas began to pray for help; witnesses said the sea calmed the instant Nicholas dropped to his knees. So important did he become to sailors that Greek and Russian seamen always sailed with an icon of Saint Nicholas.

In some parts of Europe, the legend of Saint Nicholas was incorporated into the winter solstice festivals, which later became part of our Christmas celebration. Saint Nicholas's Day had long opened the Christmas season, and as earlier chapters have described, the saint's selfless gift giving and love of children was in keeping with the themes of the Nativity. Because the holidays happen so close together, some places eventually merged the festivities. Germany and France, for example, transferred most of the activities surrounding Saint Nicholas's Eve to Christmas Eve. The majority of European countries still keep the two separate, however. Saint Nicholas brings goodies on his day, and the Christ child or the Three Wise Men deliver on Christmas or Epiphany Eve.

In some places, Saint Nicholas is also celebrated as the Boy Bishop. In England, a Boy Bishop was chosen to preside over the solstice festival, along with Saint Nick's older incarnation, Father Christmas.

❦ Festive Fact ❦

Russia's Father Frost lives beyond the Arctic Circle and arrives New Year's Day on a reindeer-pulled sleigh with his daughter, the Snow Maiden, to place presents under trees. The Norwegian Julesvenn, the Danish Julenisse, and the Swedish Jultomten are all left treats on Saint Nicholas's Eve in an effort to get them to do the same, as well as dissuade them from trickery.

SANTA TODAY Saint Nicholas came to America by way of the Dutch in the 1600s. Sinter Claes, as the name was rendered, was obviously an important figure to the Dutch settlers. They named their first church in the New World the Saint Nicholas Collegiate Church, even though it was Protestant.

In the Dutch settlement of New Amsterdam—later New York City—Saint Nicholas Day and Christmas were celebrated in a merry fashion unknown to the rest of the colonies. Because of the strictly Puritan background of most of the New World settlers, any celebration of saints or Christmas was unheard of.

Illegal in New England until 1681, Christmas was later observed in the strictly religious sense—but it would be wrong to say that it was actually celebrated there in any meaningful way before the American Revolution. Certainly any impious foolery involving Saint Nicholas was considered beyond the pale in the region for decades after independence was won.

It was only in the years after the war that Christmas began to win slow acceptance as a cause for revelry in various regions of the United States, and only at the dawn of the nineteenth century did any meaningful references to the man we would come to call Santa Claus begin to appear. The change in the national attitude can probably be traced to two main factors: the intermarriage of the Pennsylvania Dutch with other settlers, and the influx of German immigrants to the new country. (German immigrants were perhaps the most enthusiastic celebrants of Christmas in Northern cities during this period.)

Although Washington Irving's nostalgic turn-of-the century satires of New Amsterdam society feature some of the earliest American literary treatments of the Saint Nicholas legend, the evolution from Saint Nicholas to the American Santa we are familiar with today appears to have begun at least two or three decades later. Clement C. Moore's enormously influential poem "A Visit from Saint Nicholas" was written in 1822, but it did not become widely popular until several years later. It was published anonymously, and to increasingly enthusiastic public response, until 1837, when Moore finally acknowledged authorship.

Although Moore's lines have perhaps been the most influential in forming an image of the modern Santa Claus, it is interesting to note that that name does not appear in the poem, nor do any of its variants.

Presumably the other formulations were passed over by the poet in favor of the less foreign-sounding Saint Nicholas.

❧ Looking Back ❧

Much of what we now consider as essential to Santa—such as his plumpness—first appeared in Clement C. Moore's poem "A Visit from Saint Nicholas." Moore apparently based his Saint Nick on a rotund gardener who worked for him.

Moore wrote the verses for his own children and recited the poem before his family for the first time on Christmas Eve. Although Santa has grown over the years from the elflike stature Moore assigned to him, it is from his lines that we get the first (and by far the ost influential) physical description of Santa.

Moore's portrayal of Saint Nicholas as a generous gift-giver and friend to children was, of course, an outgrowth of the legends surrounding Saint Nicholas. The influence of Irving's (often imaginative) accounts of the Dutch legend is also apparent throughout the poem. The poem's emphasis on snowy winter weather may be due to earlier traditions linking Saint Nicholas with winter cold—or to the fact that Moore himself enjoyed a white Christmas season in the year he composed the poem.

Moore was not the first to assign a reindeer to Saint Nicholas, but he was the first to set the total at eight and the first to popularize the names we now associate with the animals. They are, for the record, Dasher, Dancer, Prancer, Vixen, Comet, Cupid, Donder, and Blitzen. (Rudolph would come along later in a 1939 story by Robert L. May, who is also credited with replacing the original "Donder" with "Donner." A decade later, Gene Autry's voice solidified this Donner name swap in the famous and now-classic lyrical version of "Rudolph, the Red-Nosed Reindeer.")

Thomas Nast's 1863 illustrations for the poem "A Visit from Saint Nicholas," which went a long way toward standardizing the jolly one's physical appearance, were the turning point in Nast's career. Although his later political cartoons also won him national acclaim, Nast made a tradition of supplying fresh drawings of Santa for the annual Christmas issue of *Harper's Weekly*.

Although Nast's drawings had the greatest impact as far as standardizing the various images of Saint Nicholas into a single chubby, smiling figure, the final touches were added (or at least formalized) in the 1920s by artist Haddon Sundblom in a series of Coca Cola ads. Sundblom's Santa had red cheeks, wore a red gown with white fur trim, and radiated a rotund good cheer. Not surprisingly, he also liked the product! The ad campaign ran for thirty-five years and was revived in the 1990s.

SANTA'S MANY NAMES If a contest was ever held for the individual with the most names, Santa could be a contender for the prize. If you include all the identities of the one who bears gifts for children at Christmas, it is safe to say there are probably three dozen or more, although technically they don't all refer to the guy in the red suit; some refer to the Baby Jesus, Noël, or the Magi (in some places called the Three Kings).

Here are a few of the names Santa goes by: Christkindli (Switzerland), Kriss Kringle (Germany), Old Man Christmas (Chile and also Finland), Kanakaloka (Hawaii), Julenisse (Norway), Sinter Klaas (Netherlands), Santa no ojisan (Japan), Father Christmas (England), Pere Noël (France), Jouluvana (Estonia), Grandfather Frost or Dedushka Moroz (Russia), Weihnachtsmann (Austria), Sveti Nickola (Serbia and Croatia), Babbo Natale (Italy), Kerstman (Holland), and San Nicolás (Mexico).

WHICH WAY TO SANTA CLAUS, INDIANA? Proof of Santa's early popularity in the United States can be found in the Indiana town of Santa Claus, named by Swiss colonists back in 1852. Legend has it that this naming occurred on Christmas Eve. As the townspeople sat in their new church contemplating names, children began to yell "Santa Claus," and the name took. By the 1940s, the Santa Claus post office was flooded with mail addressed to Santa, the person. Far from being dismayed by this daunting flow of correspondence, the town welcomed the attention, although volunteers often had to be recruited to help handle the large volume. The town is a nice place to visit during the Christmas season, with its Kris Kringle Street, a twenty-three-foot-high statue of Santa, and a Santa Claus park.

In 1949, the first of many Santa theme parks was set up. The North Pole Village, located in Wilmington, New York, opened for business complete with reindeer, toy workshop, and post office. It is still in operation, a popular tourist spot during its June 1 to November 1 season.

There is actually a University of Santa Claus; it trains department store Santas. Graduates receive a Bs.C., Bachelor of Santa Clausery. Similar, though not quite as catchy, is the one-day training school for store Santas run by Western Temporary Services in California. Potential Santas must meet physical and performance requirements and pass a strict background check. After graduating, Santas must abide by a code of conduct to ensure the safety of the children and protect the sanctity of the figure they portray. Some of the more interesting guidelines are as follows:

- Bathe daily, using a strong deodorant and mouthwash.
- Clean the beard and gloves nightly to keep them white.
- Don't leave the Santa seat, even if a child vomits or has "an accident."
- Don't say "Ho, ho, ho!"; it may frighten children.
- Don't flirt with the elves.
- When it comes time to take a bathroom break, say, "Santa is going to feed the reindeer."

And so Saint Nicholas has made his way from Asia Minor to American department stores—undergoing a few alterations on the way.

Indeed, it is extremely doubtful whether Saint Nicholas would recognize himself in Santa Claus if the two were to come face to face today. Still, perhaps somewhere, somehow, Saint Nicholas is aware of the joy his existence has brought to children, and children at heart, everywhere. After all, if it were not for this quietly devout and generous man, there would be no Santa Claus. And who could imagine Christmas without Santa?

WHY DOES SANTA RIDE A REINDEER-DRIVEN SLEIGH?

The popularity of Santa and his reindeer is largely due to Clement C. Moore, who put the two together in his wildly successful poem, "A Visit from Saint Nicholas." But Moore was not the first to pair Santa with hoofed friends. Before Moore published his poem, a number of less successful books had portrayed Santa flying around in a sleigh pulled by one reindeer. This concept had long been popular in Russia, where Father Frost arrived in the villages in a reindeer-drawn sleigh. The Norse god Wodin was said to ride his horse Sleipner through the air to make sure people were behaving; in Holland, Saint Nicholas rides Sleipner to this day.

Today, Rudolph the Red-Nosed Reindeer is by far the most popular of Santa's nine; he is also the youngest (or at any rate the most recent arrival). Moore introduced the first eight reindeer in 1823; Rudolph did not come along until 1939, in a story by Robert L. May. Rudolph's notoriety owes much to the popularity of the Gene Autry song "Rudolph the Red-Nosed Reindeer," released in 1949 and a holiday classic to this day.

⌒﹏◦﹏⌒

WHY A RED SUIT? Think bishop's cape and you have the answer. Nicholas, who was also known as Nicholas of Smyrna, Nicholas of Myra, and Hagios Nikolaos, was the bishop of the church at Smyrna (Izmir in modern Turkey). He lived during the fourth century and was known to be kind and generous to children, especially the very poor, giving away his wealth to them. Tradition states that he tossed special little gifts or bags of gold to them through open windows or down chimneys.

Although Thomas Nast is widely credited with creating the first image of Santa in the mid-1800s, Louis Prang put a red suit on Santa Claus for a Christmas card he created in 1885. Perhaps he knew about the color of the cape worn by Saint Nicholas. Anyway, Prang continued with the red-suited Santa in cards for the following year. Prior to 1931, American artist Norman Rockwell painted various versions of Santa. Most verged on saintly visions of the old elf. In the 1920s, the Coca Cola Company used images of Santa similar to those created by Nast to sell its product. But in 1931, a man named Haddon Sundblom developed a Santa image for Coca Cola that would become the company's standard for the next thirty or so years. At first Sundblom used his friend Lou Prentice as a model until Prentice died. Then Sundblom used his own image to create a standardized version of Santa Claus, the one whose features and size we know today. And yes, Sundblom's Santa always wears the red suit.

❧⚬❧

THE WOMAN BEHIND THE WONDER: MRS. CLAUS

The man in the red suit can at times be extremely exuberant and a little too jolly for his own good. But he married a wonderful woman, Mrs. Claus, who appears to be as constant as the North Star, as patient as a saint, and as loving as an angel.

WHY DOES *Santa* WEAR RED?

Santa's wife was first mentioned in 1888, in the magazine *Wide Awake*. She was called "Goody Santa Claus," which was a contraction in the vernacular of that period for "good wife." Today, she is called simply Mrs. Claus. Mrs. Claus can do almost anything except guide the sleigh, handle the reindeer, or slide down the chimney. She would definitely need some trousers for that, and Mrs. Claus doesn't seem to own any! Some would call her a little old fashioned. She's also never owned a pair of stilettos, carried a designer handbag, worn a bustier, or used Botox.

Santa likes the way she keeps her white hair swept up into a bun and doesn't mind that she's plump. He appreciates her cooking and her sense of orderliness because he knows that Mrs. Claus is the one who keeps the North Pole humming along. She is the love of Santa's life, if you don't count cookies.

SHOULD SANTA'S COOKIES BE LOW FAT? The first images of Santa, created more than a century ago, show a man who is definitely leaner than he appears to be in more recent representations. Like many people who are taking in more calories than they need, Santa's eating habits may be starting to show up as a little spread around the middle. Blame it on his diet . . . okay, the cookies. Perhaps he could replace those icebox butter cookies, Pfferneuse, krumkake, and Melt-Aways with some tasty treats a tad lower in fat, say a lemon or poppy-seed biscotti or some *lebkuchen* (gingerbread).

Those traditional rich Christmas cookies had their origin in medieval European kitchens, where the ingredients were all natural and were mostly found just outside the kitchen door. People did not have the modern conveniences that we have today. They probably worked off the calories of a butter cookie in under an hour. So unless Santa gets a gift certificate to a gym for Christmas, he'd better start thinking of other exercise options, or in another century that sleigh may not get airborne. Can you say "low-calorie cookie"?

DOES SANTA NEED A GPS? A global positioning system could help Santa reorient the sleigh if he ever gets confused about landmarks. It might be a good idea for him to get one of these gadgets, in light of all the talk about climate changes due to global warming. Land Mass and familiar landscapes can shift anywhere in the world. Warmer temperatures could cause the seas to rise. Pieces of a polar ice shelf could break away from a larger mass.

Santa's Village at the North Pole is located in the middle of the Artic Ocean (unlike the South Pole, which is on land). It's dark twenty-four hours a day in the winter at the North Pole, and it's mighty cold (winter temps range between minus 43 degrees Fahrenheit to minus 15). The sea at the North Pole is always frozen to a depth of two to three yards; however, reports about the recent climate change and the decrease in ice thickness could be problematic for Santa, Mrs. Claus, and the Eves. Santa's Village might be on thin ice.

One hopes, of course, that it would never float off to where Santa and the reindeer couldn't find it. Mrs. Claus has probably given this a good deal of thought and is already preparing, so no need to worry. Besides, those reindeer have an uncanny sense of direction.

WHY DOES *Santa* WEAR RED?

WHY DOES SANTA FLY THE POLAR ROUTE? The short answer is that it that flying the polar route shaves time off Santa's long trip around the world on Christmas Eve. There are numerous variations on cross-polar routings that Santa could take. He has many things to consider—the weight of the sleigh, the weather, the condition of his reindeer, and the number of stops he has to make, among them. Each year Mrs. Claus helps him do all the calculations before take-off, and she encourages him to stick to the schedule. She is his air traffic controller and monitors the progress of the sleigh from a command center in Santa's Village.

An interesting aside is that the North Pole has always been designated international territory, which means that no one country can claim Santa as its citizen. The people of Finland, however, believe that the North Pole is in their country, just north of the Artic Circle. The people of Greenland say that the people of Finland are wrong and that the North Pole is actually in Greenland. More recently, the Canadians have asserted their sovereignty, saying that their boundaries now stretch to the North Pole. But Citizen Santa belongs to the world.

〜◦〜

COMING DOWN THE CHIMNEY Santa's favorite way to enter the house is to slide down the chimney. It derives from the poem of Clement C. Moore, "A Visit from Saint Nicholas." One verse refers to Saint Nicholas coming down the chimney. Moore's story may have inspired Thomas Nast to paint Santa Claus in what has become one of the most popular images of the jolly old man.

SO WHERE DO ALL THE LETTERS GO? It is likely that children's letters to Santa will end up in Santa Claus, Indiana. The town has only 2,000 residents, and yet its post office handles thousands of letters annually during Christmastime. And while we are on the subject, the U.S. Postal Service has official guidelines for writing to Santa. Letters must be addressed to "Santa" and on the next line followed by the letter writer's local city's name, state, and zip code. Children should ask their parents to help them correctly spell the words in the address. The U.S. Postal Service requests that children not mail candy, cookies, or hay for the reindeer in their envelopes.

THE ORIGINS OF RUDOLPH AND HIS RED NOSE

Robert May worked as a copywriter for Montgomery Ward. The store needed a new "giveaway" to bring families with children in to do their holiday shopping. In 1939, as his wife lay dying of cancer, May wrote the story of Rudolph. Though he was technically under assignment from Montgomery Ward, the story was really for his little daughter Barbara.

After his wife passed away, May found himself deeply in debt. He went to his employer to get the rights to the Rudolph story reassigned to him. The employer gave permission, and May published the story commercially in 1947. His brother-in-law, Johnny Marks, was a songwriter. Marks changed the story slightly to make it work as a song and called it "Rudolph the Red-Nosed Reindeer." When the popular cowboy actor, Gene Autry sang it in 1949, it became an instant hit.

WHY DOES *Santa* WEAR RED?

First at Thanksgiving?: "Jingle Bells"

"Jingle Bells," by John Pierpont (1785–1866)

Dashing through the snow,
In a one-horse open sleigh,
O'er the fields we go,
Laughing all the way;
Bells on bobtail ring,
Making spirits bright,
What fun it is to laugh and sing
A sleighing song tonight!

Jingle bells, jingle bells,
Jingle all the way!
Oh, what fun it is to ride
In a one-horse open sleigh!

Jingle bells, jingle bells,
Jingle all the way!
Oh, what fun it is to ride
In a one-horse open sleigh!

You may be surprised to learn that "Jingle Bells" was composed in 1857 (or possibly before) by James Lord Pierpont for the Thanksgiving celebration of his Boston Sunday School class (although when the song was copyrighted in 1857, Pierpont was an organist for a church in Savannah, Georgia). Supposedly, the song was so well received that it was used again for the Christmas celebration. Children especially seem to connect with the song. It lends itself to accompaniment of bells, long associated with Santa in his sleigh guided by reindeer. On December 16, 1965, the Gemini 6 astronauts made it the first carol to be broadcast from space when they played a rendition of it on bells and a harmonica that they had sneaked onboard the spacecraft.

WHY DOES *Santa* WEAR RED?

part six

deck the halls

ny room—kitchen, bathroom, sundeck—is fair game for Christmas decorating, not just the room where the tree is. And don't forget the outside of the house! Couldn't the porch, windows, mailboxes, bushes, and even the shrubs benefit from a bit of colorful holiday decorating? Between nature and your own ingenuity, you should discover ample means of decking those halls (and yards). Come along for the ride as we discover new and traditional ways to decorate your house from floor to ceiling, ground to sky!

WHY DOES *Santa* WEAR RED?

THE HISTORY OF DECORATING The tradition of decorating with evergreens can be traced back to ancient times, when people brought branches into their dwellings to shelter and warm nature spirits. They returned the branches to nature when they observed that the days were growing longer and buds on trees were beginning to swell. The Mesopotamians loved fringe and adorned bushes with it. The ancient Romans celebrated the holiday of Saturnalia with evergreen decorations.

The early Christian church disapproved of the decorating of houses to mark the Nativity of Jesus. By the third century, the practice was disallowed, perhaps out of the belief that it was too much like pagan ritual. Yet by the fifth century, the Feast of the Nativity, as Christmas was then called, had evolved into a favorite holiday, and greenery was again seen in homes of Christians.

In the Middle Ages, long after Christianity had replaced the old pagan rituals and traditions, people still believed that the green leafy boughs they brought inside their houses contained tree spirits that could be mischievous if not returned to nature. Mistletoe, holly, and evergreens were the favorite greens used by the medieval people. They made a hoop of greenery (any kind, including box, yew, and rosemary), tying it around a pliant willow branch to make a "holy bough."

The holy bough was blessed by a priest and then hung from a beam just beyond the doorway of the home. A kiss under the bough symbolized both a kiss of peace and a burying of old grudges. The holy bough became known by the eighteenth century as the "holly bough."

Despite its original significance, some saw the bough as a vulgar display and an affront to the holiness of Christmas. In England, the holly bough was banned for a few years. Kisses beneath it were stolen, and thus a new tradition was born—that is, the plucking of holly berries from the bough until they were all removed, marking the end of the kisses as well.

An illustration from the 1500s shows an image of Saint Christopher with the Christ child upon his shoulders passing under a tree without leaves but laden with fruit, candy, and some kind of balls. Could it have been a forerunner of the decorated Christmas tree?

During the next century in America, the swing of the Christmas pendulum swung back. The Puritans refused to observe Christmas as a holiday, and conservative Bostonians outlawed it. But in 1870, Christmas became an official holiday in the United States. In Germany during the 1800s, people decorated greenery with apples and lavishly covered their Christmas trees with paper streamers, real fruit, ornaments, and candles.

Gradually, the German passion for holiday decorations made its way to England and America, where the decorating of homes during December evolved into a favorite family activity. The twentieth century witnessed the increasing popularity of artificial greens and trees and decorations from virtually every culture of the world. Decorating ideas for Christmas are now the mainstay of December television shows and magazine articles. Christmas decorating has become a high art.

✎❍✎

WHY DOES *Santa* WEAR RED?

SHOPPING IN YOUR OWN BACK YARD Your own back yard is one big shopping opportunity when it comes to great Christmas decorations. Here are some simple suggestions:

- Collect pine or other branches and pinecones from the woods or a nearby park and bring them inside to decorate windowsills, fireplace mantels, or other appropriate places in your home.
- Decorate the house with extra branches from the Christmas tree. Find some mistletoe to hang not so discreetly in the arch of a doorway.
- Stock up on that traditional Christmas plant, the poinsettia. Place them anywhere and everywhere!
- Use holly boughs to create a large arch over your front door. Begin by standing large branches at each side of the door and build up the branches with greenery using tacks.
- Make a natural garland for your Christmas tree with pinecones, berries, or other natural and colorful ingredients.

$\gtrsim\!\!\sim\!\!\circ\!\!\sim\!\!\sim$

WE ALL NEED SOMETHING TO ROCK AROUND
Whether you buy your tree from a roadside stand, unwrap it from a box purchased at a department store (often the choice of those who find themselves short on space), or trek to your own private grove to chop one down yourself, you'll want to pick one that's right for your living space. Measure the floor-to-ceiling dimension of your selected room before you select a

tree, and be sure to leave a good bit of space at the top for the angel, star, or other major ornament.

Assuming yours is a live tree, you should mount the base of the tree in a little water to reduce the risk of fire. (Most good stands have a water well that will not leak.) Before you set up the Christmas tree stand, however, place a layer of newspaper underneath it, topped with some red or green tissue paper on which to place the gifts.

Your selection of tree decorations is best left to your own tastes and family tradition. Note, though, that there are a number of good ideas later in this chapter for specific homemade holiday crafts projects; many are suitable for the tree.

TWINKLE LIGHTS DELIGHT In 1882, an associate of Thomas Edison named Edward Johnson thought it would be a good idea to have a little string of electric lights to use on Christmas trees. Since the middle of the seventeenth century, people had been bringing fresh green trees into their homes on Christmas Eve and carefully affixing small candles to the branches with pins or a little wax. However, as you can imagine, the fire risk was great. Johnson put his idea into practice by wiring eighty bulbs together and draping them onto a tree.

The challenges of stringing some lights on the tree, however, were great. General Electric could provide hand-blown bulbs, but no one really understood how to wire them together. Wiremen had to be hired by homeowners to make the bulbs work. Finally, in 1903, the American Eveready

Company produced a set of lights with bulbs that screwed in and plugged conveniently into a wall socket.

But some people still used candles. A tragic New York City fire in 1917 gave Albert Sadacca, the teenage son of Spanish immigrants, the idea for selling Christmas tree lights to the American public. He only sold about a hundred sets of clear lights in the first year, but when he painted color onto the lights, sales exploded. Up until 1965, Albert's company—NOMA Electric Company—was the world's largest Christmas lighting company.

～≫◦≪～

WREATHS GALORE The most popular wreaths are those made from pine branches and holly berries. Wreaths are easy to make and present virtually limitless possibilities when it comes to decorating.

To make a wreath, you need a frame. This can be either two untwisted coat hangers or, if you can find them, switches of willow. Make a circular frame about one foot in diameter. For an evergreen wreath, tie small branches of evergreen to the frame with wire, building around the wreath until it's as full as desired. Decorate with berries, pinecones, or a simple ribbon.

You might also want to try wreaths that feature dried and polished (lacquered) fruit and nuts; just fruit; just nuts; pinecones and greenery; candy; cotton balls; miniature glass ornaments and dried flowers; or any combination of these. Try adorning a wreath with toy musical instruments, or embellish one with only angels. Twist wire-edged gold or silver ribbon around a decorated wreath and tie the ends into a festive bow. Or make miniature cornucopias out of sheet music. Fashion a little handle out of paper or ribbon. Glue a lacy gold doily edging around the top and fill with sprigs of holly or wrapped candies. Attach them to your wreath for a romantic Victorian look.

SO SANTA WILL SEE: INDOOR DECORATING TIPS

Create a festive holiday display by grouping miniature conical evergreen trees (either real ones, purchased from garden centers, or fake ones from craft stores) and place them into pretty little boxes or containers. Decorate each one so that it reflects a theme. For example, use only snowflakes on one tree. Or hang paper cutouts of Victorian characters. Or find different images or faces of Santa, and make that the focus. Use charms (like crosses and hearts) from old bracelets, or cover the tree with tiny red ribbons that you tie or glue on with a hot glue gun. Don't forget to embellish the containers. Glue star-shaped medallions onto the boxes and finish with trim (by gluing on lace or other types of trim from a fabric store) around the top edge of the planter box.

Find and decorate a sleigh centerpiece using ribbon, holly, miniature boxes wrapped like Christmas presents, and gold- and silver-wrapped candies. Place

WHY DOES *Santa* WEAR RED?

candles into inexpensive tall brass candlesticks, and tie ribbon and fake fruit and berries around the top of the candle holder (just beneath where the candle anchors into the candlestick). This arrangement will not only look beautiful, it will be the perfect area to place Santa's cookies and milk.

For some paper-white narcissus or freesia bulbs, simply place the bulb on top of some glass marbles that you've poured into a cylindrical vase. Tie it with red, green, or candy-stripe ribbon. Add water up to the base of the bulb and maintain that water level over the next few weeks until the bulb grows and blooms. When the blooming cycle is over, throw the bulb away.

Place old Christmas cards and pictures of Santa that are reminiscent of Christmases past on a table (like a coffee table) and cover it with glass so you can enjoy the cards without damaging them. Or as you receive new cards, tape them around your door or display them on an entry table.

Hang a collection of Christmas stockings or set out a collection of Christmas books. Fill a pretty lace-draped basket with shiny Christmas ball ornaments. Make a special place to display religious symbols that are important to you and your family. Perhaps drape a table with new cloth and add pillar candles of varying heights. Put out icons or pictures of the Madonna and Child or a small Nativity scene or objects that carry special Christmas significance.

Drape greenery over your fireplace mantel and add pedestal candles and poinsettias. Make a long garland of evergreens and drape it around a tall narrow window to look like its frame, or using multiple garlands of artificial greenery to wrap your stairway banister. Tie on Christmas plaid ribbon and pretty fake fruit that has been glazed and glittered, or burnish the fruit yourself with mica powders (available from craft stores) along with clumps of berries, and pinecones. Then, to create a wonderful holiday ambiance, wrap colored twinkle-lights the length of the banister.

With your children, grandchildren, or the kids in the neighborhood, make a gingerbread house (from kits available at kitchen stores in early December). Set aside a special place to display it. Pieces of the house often disappear during the holidays as hungry friends and family members find themselves unable to resist the urge to nibble on it.

Make a spray of fresh eucalyptus and bay and laurel leaves. The fragrance is wonderful. Tie with ribbon and hang it on your front door to create a festive entry.

AND TO ALL, A GOOD NIGHT: OUTDOOR ORNAMENTS Icicle lights are beautiful along the roofline of houses, but so are clear twinkle lights around laurel wreaths on the front door, in the birches standing in the front yard, or on the gate of the walkway. Put pretty poinsettias in a mass on the porch at the front door. Hang sprays of greenery tied with ribbon at the base of porch lights. Create a festive birdhouse (think craft store for the house) by adding ribbon and seed pods, dried herbs and leaves, whole nuts, and edible berries. The birds will love you for it. Create a Nativity scene in a corner of your yard. Hang bells with ribbon from trees to create a soft tinkle in the wind.

The Making of a Mozart Duet: "Deck the Halls with Boughs of Holly"

"Deck the Halls with Boughs of Holly," traditional Welsh song

Deck the halls with boughs of holly,
Falalalala, lalalala;
'Tis the season to be jolly,
Falalalala, lalalala.
Don we now our gay apparel,
Falala, falala, lalala.
Troll the ancient yuletide carol,
Falalalala, lalalala.

See the blazing yule before us,
Falalalala, lalalala;
Strike the harp and join the chorus
Falalalala, lalalala.
Follow me in merry measure,
Falala, falala, lalala.
While I sing of Christmas treasure,
Falalalala, lalalala.

Fast away the old year passes,
Falalalala, lalalala;
Hail the new, ye lads and lasses,
Falalalala, lalalala.
Sing we joyous songs together,
Falala, falala, lalala.
Heedless of the wind and weather,
Falalalala, lalalala.

In the eighteenth century, this popular tune was used by Mozart for a piano and violin duet. The words are American, but the melody belongs to a Welsh winter song known as "Nos Galan." The repetitive fa-la-la portions were most likley meant to be plucked on a harp and were a popular feature of medieval ballads and madrigal songs. Although J. P. McCaskey served as the editor of the song collection that published the lyrics, and his name sometimes appears as the lyricist, he did not write the original words.

all the little things we do

*W*hy do we kiss under mistletoe? Where did the Christmas tree originate? Who printed the first Christmas card? Why do we leave gifts in stockings? When did Santa get his reindeer? We are all used to participating in the traditions of the season, but do we even know why we do all these silly things? Well, you're about to learn! In this part we will look at those traditions that are engrained in us and figure out where they came from and why we love to participate.

WHY DO WE WRITE "X"-MAS? The "X" in Xmas stands for the Greek letter chi, the first letter in the Greek word for Christ. Over time, the letter "X" came to stand for the name of Christ. The practice gained very wide usage in the mass media during the twentieth century—but not, as many erroneously believe, because of any squeamishness about using the word "Christmas." Often, Xmas simply fits better in a headline.

<hr />

COLORS OF THE SEASON: RED AND GREEN Why are red and green the colors of Christmas? No one really knows for sure, but there have been plenty of educated guesses. Green is the easier of the two to theorize about; it is the color of the evergreens that symbolize so much that is important to the meaning of the holiday. (See Chapter 42 on the history of Christmas decorating, which gives a full account of the importance of greenery in the early Christmas festivals.) The holly berry seems to be responsible for the red. This red berry lives through winter, thus symbolizing life in the face of death, a representation of Christ.

<hr />

BABY JESUS IS EVERYWHERE The first Nativity scene was created at the church of Santa Maria Maggiore in tenth-century Rome. The custom was soon popular at other churches, each one constructing ornate mangers with gold, silver, jewels, and precious stones. Though popular among high society, such opulence was far removed from the original circumstances of Christ's birth, as well as being inaccessible to the poorer masses.

We owe the crèche to Saint Francis of Assisi, who revised the gaudier displays of his time. In 1224, Saint Francis sought to remedy these problems by creating the first manger scene that was true to the biblical account of Christ's birth. Called a crèche, the scene that Saint Francis set up for the village of Greccio was made up of hay, carved figures, and live animals. For the unlettered people of the town, it captured more of the spirit and the story of Christ's birth than any splendid art treasure.

The popularity of the crèche spread throughout the world. In Italy it is called a *presepio*; in Germany, a *Krippe*. It is a *naciemiento* in Spain and Latin America, a *jeslicky* in the Czech Republic, a *pesebre* in Brazil, and a *portal* in Costa Rica.

ANOTHER POINSETTIA? The legend of the plant we now associate so strongly with Christmas arose years ago in Mexico, where it was traditional to leave gifts on the altar for Jesus on Christmas Eve. As the story goes, among a group of worshipers one night was a poor boy who had no present to leave for Jesus. Upset by his inability to provide a gift, the boy knelt outside the church window and prayed. In the spot where he knelt, there sprung a beautiful plant with vibrant red leaves. In Mexico this plant is called "the Flower of the Holy Night."

Today, Encinitas, California, is called the Poinsettia Capital of the World because of the large number of poinsettias found there.

✿ Looking Back ✿

The first American ambassador to Mexico, Dr. Joel Roberts Poinsett (appointed 1825–
1829), was impressed by the vibrant plant Mexicans called the Flower of the Holy
Night. He brought it to America, where it was subsequently renamed in his honor.

STOCKINGS HUNG BY THE CHIMNEY WITH CARE

The idea of hanging stockings out on Christmas Eve is believed to have come from Amsterdam, where children leave out their shoes on Saint Nicholas's Eve in hopes that he will fill them with goodies. But where did the people of Amsterdam get the idea? Perhaps from Saint Nicholas himself. One of the most popular stories surrounding the saint concerns his generosity to the three daughters of a poor family. It seems the daughters were of marriageable age, but they could not marry because they had no dowry. Nicholas heard of their plight and set out to help them. In the middle of the night (to keep his act secret), Nicholas threw bags of gold coins down the girls' chimney. The bags landed in the girl's stockings, which they had hung out to dry.

TRIMMING THE TREE
The Christmas tree is by far the most popular form of greenery in the United States. Indeed, it has become such an integral part of our Christmas celebration that most people cannot imagine

WHY DOES *Santa* WEAR RED?

celebrating the holiday without one in their living room. Yet like much we associate with Christmas, the tree is a relatively recent innovation.

The decorated Christmas tree apparently had no broad popularity in colonial America. The tradition, followed by German immigrants for years, did not catch on in other parts of society until the 1830s. It is said that the Hessians defeated by George Washington in the Battle of Trenton in 1776 may have been observing the holiday in the custom of their homeland by setting lighted candles upon the boughs of a tree.

No one seems to be able to explain the reasons behind the popularity of the Christmas tree, but along with Santa, it is now the most common secular entity associated with Christmas in the United States. For most of us, the tree's attractiveness needs no explanation. The beauty, the smell, the fun of decorating, the spirit, the memories of holidays past—whether of pine, fir, or cedar, there is simply nothing like a good Christmas tree.

As early as the Roman Saturnalia, trees were hung with decorations, but this custom did not become part of Christmas until the Middle Ages. Like all greenery with pagan origins, the tree has long been assigned Christian significance, but how it came to be so important to Christmas is the subject of much debate. The earliest record of a decorated tree is from an English book printed in 1441, which describes a tree set up in the middle of a village, decorated with ivy. The popular consensus, however, is that the Christmas tree as we know it originated in Germany.

According to one legend, Saint Boniface, who helped organize the Christian church in France and Germany during the mid-700s, was responsible for the first Christmas tree. One Christmas Eve, Saint Boniface was

WHY DOES *Santa* WEAR RED?

traveling through the forest and happened upon a group of people gathered around an oak tree preparing to sacrifice a child to the god Thor. In protest of this act, Saint Boniface destroyed the oak, either with an ax or a single blow from his fist. In any event, when the oak was felled, a fir tree appeared in its place. Saint Boniface informed the people that this was the Tree of Life, representing Christ.

Another familiar legend holds that when Christ was born, all the animals received the power to speak and the trees bloomed and brought forth fruit, despite the harsh winter. All the grand trees came forth to pay homage to the Lord, except one tiny fir tree, embarrassed by her stature. But then the Lord came down and lighted the fir tree's branches, making her sparkle, and she was no longer ashamed.

Though these legends are entertaining, most experts believe that the truth behind the Christmas tree is much less spectacular. In the fourteenth and fifteenth centuries, pine trees were used in Europe as part of the miracle plays performed in front of cathedrals at Christmas time. The plays detailed the birth and fall of humanity, its salvation through the death and resurrection of Christ, and Christ's promise of redemption. The pine trees, decorated with apples, symbolized the Tree of Life in the Garden of Eden.

Though such plays were later banned by the church, the tradition of this Paradise Tree, or *Paradeisbaum,* was kept alive in individual homes. People began decorating the trees with wafers to represent the Eucharist. Later, these wafers evolved into cookies, cakes, fruit, and other goodies. At first these foods were shaped to represent some aspect of the Nativity, but in time they came to depict anything the decorator's heart desired.

To this day, the Christmas tree enjoys incredible popularity in Germany. The decorating of the tree is one of the most anticipated events of the holiday, and in some homes each family member has his or her own tree. So beloved is the Christmas tree in Germany that the most popular carol there after "Silent Night" is "O, Tannenbaum" ("Oh, Christmas Tree").

By the 1800s, the Christmas tree had spread to Norway, Finland, Sweden, Denmark, and Austria. In Scandinavia, fishermen of old trimmed their trees with fishnets and flags. Today it is more common in those countries to decorate with cookies, candy, fruit, lighted candles, and flags.

The most famous tree in Great Britain is a gift each year from Norway, in appreciation for Britain's help to them during World War II. When Norway was under Nazi occupation, King Haakan set up a free Norwegian government in London. Every year since 1947, Norway has presented the people of Britain with an enormous tree at least seventy feet high, which is set up in Trafalgar Square for all to enjoy.

🌿 Festive Fact 🌿

Popular with wealthy Americans around the end of the nineteenth century were combination tree-stands and music boxes. These rotated the tree and played soothing music.

In America, the Christmas tree caught on in the nineteenth century and has become almost as beloved as it is in Germany. Most homes have some type of Christmas tree during the holidays; trees can also be found everywhere from department stores to offices to churches. Even trees growing outside are decorated.

WHY DOES *Santa* WEAR RED?

SPECIAL TOUCHES: ORNAMENTS, HOLLY, IVY, AND MISTLETOE

SPECIAL TOUCHES: ORNAMENTS, HOLLY, IVY, AND MISTLETOE The earliest Christmas ornaments consisted of edible goodies, typically fruits and nuts. Eventually, these made way for cookies, candy, and cakes. Flowers and paper decorations provided inedible beauty.

The first commercial ornaments for Christmas trees were actually hollow, brightly colored containers that held good things to eat. The most popular of these was probably the cornucopia.

When the goodies got too heavy for the tree, German glassblowers began manufacturing the first glass ornaments. But these and other purely decorative elements would not be the main attraction of the Christmas tree for some years. (Originally, trees were the means by which presents were displayed on Christmas morning before their owners claimed them. Small toys, candies, and other treats were hung on the boughs; children would awaken and strip the tree.) But today, Christmas wouldn't be Christmas without holly, ivy, and mistletoe! So let's see how each of these great decorative traditions developed.

Holly

In ancient times, holly was thought to be magical because of its shiny leaves and its ability to bear fruit in winter. Some believed it contained a syrup that cured coughs, while others hung it over their beds to produce good dreams. Holly was a popular Saturnalia gift among the Romans. The Romans later brought holly to England, where it was also considered sacred. In medieval times, holly, along with ivy, became the subject of many Christmas songs. Some of these songs assigned a sex to the holly and ivy (holly is male, ivy female), while other, more religious, songs and poems portray the holly berry as a symbol of Christ.

Ivy

In pagan times, ivy was closely associated with Bacchus, the god of wine, and it played a big part in all festivals in which he figured. English tavern-keepers eventually adopted ivy as a symbol and featured it on their signs. Its festive past has not kept ivy from being incorporated into modern Christian celebrations, however.

Mistletoe

To this day, mistletoe—a parasitic plant that grows on oak and other deciduous trees—is the only form of greenery not allowed inside a Christian church during the holiday season. Although other greenery was also used in pagan festivals, mistletoe was actually worshiped.

Both druids and Romans considered the plant sacred, as a healing plant and a charm against evil. Because it grew without roots, as if by magic, mistletoe was thought to be the connection between Earth and the heavens. Mistletoe was also considered a symbol of peace. Warring soldiers who found themselves under mistletoe quickly put down their weapons and made a temporary truce. In a related custom, ancient Britons hung mistletoe in their doorways to keep evil away. Those who entered the house safely were given a welcome kiss.

While the custom of kissing under the mistletoe lost popularity in most other countries, it remained popular in England and the United States. Today, most consider mistletoe an excuse for kissing and nothing more. In France, however, some people still brew it into a tea as a cure for stomachaches.

BRAVING THE COLD: CAROL SINGERS The tradition of singing carols hearkens back to the Middle Ages, when Nativity plays were popular. In Slovakia, carolers carried a small homemade Nativity scene from one cottage to the next and from village to village, where the groups would sing for their neighbors. Singers had to brave inclement weather and were probably welcomed into the houses to warm themselves before proceeding to their next stop. The figures in their Nativities were made from carved wood and colored paintings on paper. In their homes, carolers might have a much larger Nativity display, around which the family would gather to sing sacred songs of Christmas. The singing of songs evolved into beautiful music called *pastorale* that addressed the gifts of nature that the Wise Men also presented to the Christ Child. The tradition of *pastorales* during the season of Advent continues in Christmas concerts throughout the country of Slovakia.

In the United Kingdom, carolers brave the cold to sing in public in order to raise money for charity. Carol services are held there as well. One of the most famous is held in the chapel of King's College in Cambridge. It is called the Festival of Nine Lessons and Carols and is so popular that it is broadcast on both television and radio.

Down under in Melbourne, people gather on Christmas Eve to sing carols outdoors by candlelight. The Aussies usually have a warm December (summer there), so they don't have to brave to cold like carolers in northern climates!

CHRISTMAS CARDS FOR ALL TO SHARE The distinction of having created the first Christmas card is usually given to John Calcott Horsley, but there are some who disagree. Horsley printed his card in 1843 for Sir Henry Cole, the friend who had given him the idea. The card looked much like a postcard and consisted of three panels. The central panel pictured the typical English family of the day enjoying the holiday; this panel caused some controversy, as it showed a child drinking wine. The other panels depicted acts of charity, so important to the Victorian Christmas spirit. The card's inscription read "Merry Christmas and a Happy New Year to You." A thousand copies of the card were printed, selling for one shilling apiece.

But around the same time as Horsley, two other men, W. A. Dobson and Reverend Edward Bradley, were designing cards and sending them to their friends. These cards, however, were hand-created instead of printed.

Christmas cards soon became the popular means of sending holiday greetings among the Victorians. Most of the cards were not particularly religious. The onset of the penny post in 1840 made it affordable for people to send greetings by mail, and the invention of the steam press made Mass production possible. At one time in Britain the post office delivered on Christmas Day, which is when most people received their cards. As could be expected, this process soon became too much for postal workers, who eventually got the day off.

Across the water, in America, the Christmas card was popularized by the firm of Marcus Ward & Co., and later by Louis Prang, a German-born printer and lithographer. Prang first turned his talents toward Christmas cards in 1875, designing and printing them from his Roxbury, Massachusetts, shop. Prang created "chromos," as he called the colored lithographs, in eight colors. His cards depicted Nativity scenes, family Christmas gatherings, nature scenes, and, later, Santa. The beauty of Prang's cards did much to ensure their popularity, but so did his marketing technique. Prang would hold contests all across the country, offering prizes for the best card designs, which spurred public interest. Prang's cards went strong until 1890, when U.S. buyers began importing cheaper cards from German manufacturers. Americans reclaimed the market twenty years later.

⌢⊙⌢

BONUSES, TIPS, AND OTHER GREEN GIFTS Department store owner F. W. Woolworth was the first to institute the Christmas bonus, in 1899. Savvy to the ever-growing fiscal importance of the Christmas shopping season, Woolworth decided to take steps to ensure that his stores ran smoothly through the frenzied buying time. Working under the assumption that happy workers are reliable and productive workers, Woolworth gave a bonus of $5 to each employee for every year of service, with bonuses not to exceed $25—quite a sum of money in those days. The holiday bonus has a cousin, the Christmas tip, extended to letter carriers, apartment complex employees, and other workers. Both are outgrowths of the English tradition of giving to the needy on Boxing Day.

The custom of giving employees the day off for Christmas was apparently not observed in the United States until about 1875. Up until that time, nearly all workers were expected to report as usual—unless the holiday fell on a Sunday, of course. (No matter the time of year, merchants were forbidden to sell their wares on the Sabbath, although some were arrested for trying to do so during the holiday season.) Store clerks of the era, paid not by the hour but the day, worked thousands of unpaid overtime hours during the holiday rush each year. Woolworth's later generosity toward them was the first in a long series of concessions by the owners of retail establishments to harried store workers.

Looking Back

In 1876, publishing magnate James Gordon Bennett, Jr., left his breakfast waiter a Christmas tip of $6,000—perhaps $200,000 in today's funds. Bennett's tip was—and is—among the most extravagant on record.

BLACK FRIDAY The day after Thanksgiving has long been considered the start of the Christmas shopping season. Small businesses and giant retailers alike use that day to lure in shoppers with special promotions and deeply discounted prices. Black Friday came by its name because retailers traditionally could make enough on that day to remain profitable ("stay in the black") for the remainder of the year. Stores do everything they can to entice hard-core shoppers to spend money in their stores. Shops typically open early and sometimes even offer coffee and doughnuts to the earliest arriving customers.

"O Holy Night": Christmas Premieres on the Radio

O holy night! the stars are brightly shining,
It is the night of our dear Saviour's birth!
Long lay the world, in sin and error pining,
'Til He appear'd, and the soul felt its worth.
A thrill of hope the weary world rejoices,
For yonder breaks a new and glorious morn!
Fall on your knees! O hear the angel voices!
O night divine, O night when Christ was born!
O night divine, O night, O night divine!

Led by the light of faith serenely beaming,
With glowing hearts by His cradle we stand.
So, led by light of a star sweetly gleaming,
Here came the wise men from the Orient land.
The King of Kings lay thus in lowly manger,
In all our trials born to be our friend;
He knows our need, to our weakness no stranger;
Behold your King! Before the Lowly bend!
Behold your King! your King! before Him bend!

In 1847, French composer Adolph Charles Adam wrote the music to the poem "Minuit, Chretiens" by Placide Cappeu. The composition subsequently became known as "O Holy Night," one of the most beautiful of all Christmas carols. Adam, prior to working on "O Holy Night" had already gained recognition for his musical scores for two ballets: *Giselle*, composed in in 1844, and *Le Corsaire*, in 1856. He also wrote thirty-nine operas. In 1855, John Sullivan Dwight, translated the lyrics into English. "O Holy Night" was played on the violin by Canadian radio broadcaster Reginald Fessenden on Christmas Eve in 1906. It may have been the first time a Christmas carol was ever broadcast over the radio.

crafty gifts for all to make

*P*erhaps it is possible to get through Valentine's Day without taping up cardboard hearts and little Cupids, through Easter without coloring eggs, or even through Halloween without dressing up. Who among us, however, can imagine letting Christmas pass by without some kind of decoration? Such decorations can and do go beyond the traditional lighted Christmas tree and store-bought Santa picture on the front door. When the season to be jolly comes around, let your surroundings show it with some of these great ideas!

DECORATIONS FROM THE KITCHEN Kitchen materials can help you come up with some unique Christmas decorations! Tie up some cinnamon sticks with a holiday bow; place this on the stove or on the mantel. The fragrance is lovely, and the look is one of old-fashioned charm.

Looking for an easy, fun way to spruce up your tree? Make a garland. All you need is a long piece of string, yarn, or twine, a needle, and your imagination. The classic, of course, is the popcorn and cranberry version, but garlands can be made out of anything: candy, raisins, or dried dates, alternated with, say, buttons or colored squares of paper. Kids love to help, but watch those needles! Best to select large, dull ones and to monitor children closely during this activity.

Try making a holiday wave bottle. You'll need white olive oil, white vinegar, green and red food coloring, and a large old clear wine bottle, complete with cork, that's had the label scrubbed off. Measure a third of a cup of each liquid. (Increase in equal proportions if your bottle seems to warrant it.) Add the red food coloring to the oil; add the green food coloring to the vinegar. Then pour both liquids into the wine bottle and secure tightly with the cork. Rock back and forth for a spectacular mingling and unmingling of colors!

✎∞◦⌒✎

CRAFTS FOR CHILDREN OF ALL AGES Children remember Christmas as a time filled with special activities and unexpected treats. Working on holiday craft projects will give kids something to remember—and make your house look bright and festive.

*****Safety reminder**: Always carefully monitor crafts activities involving children and scissors. Safety scissors are strongly suggested for all of the following activities.

Here are some simple craft ideas to bring out the artist (and the Christmas spirit) in young ones.

Construction-Paper Stockings: A Timeless Classic

You will need red construction paper, green felt, cotton balls, gold and silver glitter, glue, and scissors. Cut a stocking shape out of red construction paper. Brush some glue on the top portion of the stocking and paste down cotton balls to create the impression of fur trim. Spread glue elsewhere on the stocking and decorate with glitter and felt as desired. Use a paper punch to poke a hole in the top of the ornament. Children can cut out names from different-colored paper or write them on with markers. String with yarn to hang.

The Paper-Plate Santa: A Holiday Favorite

You will need red construction paper, a paper plate, cotton balls, colored markers or crayons, glue, and scissors. On the paper plate, draw Santa's eyes, nose, and mouth using markers or crayons. Brush some glue above his eyes and around his mouth, and paste down cotton balls to make bushy eyebrows and a beard. Cut a triangle out of red construction paper for Santa's hat. Glue the hat to the top of the drawing. Then glue one cotton ball to the tip of the hat. Let dry.

Why Does *Santa* Wear Red?

And How About a Paper-Plate Wreath?

You will need a paper plate, crayons, and other decorating goodies of your choice, such as small pieces of felt, buttons, glitter, confetti, or fabric scraps, and scissors. Cut out the center of the paper plate. Color with crayons. (Green is recommended, but if your kids feel like getting creative, we certainly won't stand in their way.) Then glue bits of holiday magic to the wreath.

The Old Familiar Construction-Paper Snowflake

The cutout snowflake has a long and distinguished history in many families. It's colorful and very easy to make. Just fold colored construction paper in quarters (or into smaller sections, depending on how intricate you want the finished snowflake to be) and cut little designs in the paper. Loop a string through one of the holes and hang. (You can also tape the flakes to a poster or wall; they're beautiful on their own, too.)

✕◦✕

HOMEMADE ORNAMENTS What better keepsake to put on the tree than an ornament you or your child made—one from your own home and your heart!

Macaroni Ornaments for Years to Come

This is a classic craft that you will enjoy putting out and looking at for years to come! You will need various types of macaroni, heavy paper or a clean, dry Styrofoam meat tray (cardboard will also do), glue, and gold spray paint (adult use only). Cut a wreath shape out of heavy paper or a Styrofoam tray. Decorate with different pieces of uncooked macaroni, gluing them down in desired spots. For variety, use a number of different shapes of macaroni. When the glue is completely dry, spray the ornament with gold paint (a grownup job). Use a paper punch to poke a hole in the top of the ornament and string with yarn to hang. We've suggested a wreath here, but of course you can customize this approach to make macaroni stockings, candy canes, trees, or whatever else you desire.

Favorite Ornaments: Pinecones and Eggs

As a bonus, these great glittering mementos of Christmas can be saved for years and years. Here's how to make them. Pour a small amount of glue onto a paper plate. Roll the pinecone around in the glue, then sprinkle the cone with colored glitter and let dry. Use a pipe cleaner to create a loop or hook at the top for hanging.

Another favorite is egg ornaments. Get an uncooked white egg, and poke a small hole in each end with a needle. (Parents will need to supervise this step.) Carefully blow into one hole; this will cause the white and yolk to come out the other. When all the material is removed, decorate the egg with glitter, paint, felt, or whatever other materials strike your fancy. One popular option is to decorate the egg with different colors of melted wax, carefully applying the wax with a toothpick.

Simple Egg-Carton Ornaments

These are simple and fun. Cut each individual compartment out of an egg carton, making a small hole at the top. (You'll thread this hole with string later on when it's time to hang the ornament.) Using markers, color the compartments. Some popular themes: faces, snowflakes, and stars. It's also fun to hang a little bell inside with ribbon or thread.

Cup Ornaments: Easy and Fun

You will need Styrofoam or paper cups, string or ribbon, crayons or markers, pictures cut out of old Christmas cards or magazines, and scissors. Turn a cup upside down and poke two small holes on either side just above the bottom. String ribbon through the holes and tie a big loop so the ornament can be hung. Then decorate the cup by coloring it, gluing down pictures from cards and magazines, or both. Feeling creative? Use glue to add glitter or pieces of colored fabric!

Cupcake-Holder Ornaments, Too

Just get hold of some cupcake papers—foil or paper, plain or decorated. Flatten them out. Decorate foil ones by drawing on the plain side with crayons or markers. Decorate the plain ones with stickers or glitter. Tape a yarn loop to the top of the ornament to hang.

Hang Onto That Styrofoam

Think twice before jettisoning that Styrofoam meat tray! Wash it clean, dry it thoroughly, and make star ornaments. Cut out star shapes, then brush on glue and sprinkle with silver or gold glitter. Using a paper punch, make a hole at the top big enough for yarn to pass through; make a loop for hanging.

PIÑATAS, CANDY SLEDS, AND HOMEMADE WRAPPING PAPER It takes a little work—and some cleanup time—but we think your children will enjoy taking whacks at a real donkey-shaped piñata for the holidays. Here's a warning: It's necessary to start this craft early, as the papier-mâché piñata must dry for several days.

Combine one-third of a cup of flour with one-quarter of a cup of water; transfer the mixture to a plastic bag and knead it to make paste. Transfer the paste to a large bowl. Now blow up a balloon. Dip dry strips of newspaper into the paste and use them to cover the balloon. Let it dry.

Meanwhile, roll some newspaper into a tight ball to form the donkey's head, and tape it to balloon. Cover the head with paper dipped in paste. For ears, use cardboard from an egg carton or a box. Tape them on the head and cover them with paper dipped in paste. For legs, use four toilet paper rolls, again wrapped with paper dipped in paste. Tape them to the body. Let the donkey dry for two days.

With poster paints, paint with bright colors, adding eyes, mouth, and other elements to the head; let dry. Once it's dry, gently cut a small hole in the top of the body section (you'll pop the balloon in the process) and then drop in candy, gum, party favors, and other treats. Use string or yarn to hang the piñata from the ceiling.

For a yummy decoration, expand your Christmas decoration list to include the makings of a candy sled, complete with all the fixings: two candy canes, one candy roll (LifeSavers, for instance), one large pack of gum (a big pack with at least fifteen sticks), and chocolate kisses. Take the pack of gum and lie it flat so that the widest part is facing up. Tape or glue one

WHY DOES *Santa* WEAR RED?

candy cane to each side of the pack, making the runners for the sled. To make the riders, tape or glue the roll of LifeSavers to the pack of gum. Tape or glue chocolate kisses to the LifeSavers roll to make head, arms, and legs, and you've got yourself a sled that will slide its way to the tummy.

Making homemade wrapping paper is another fun—and inexpensive—decorating activity. You will need one large roll of paper, crayons, markers, paint, pictures cut from magazines, glue, glitter, lace, ribbons, and anything else you think might look good as a wrapping! Roll out some paper, and then cut in appropriate-size sheets to wrap specific gifts. Try to personalize your sheets. If the person who is to receive the gift is a sports enthusiast, adorn the wrapping paper with images clipped from *Sports Illustrated*. It's best to carefully glue the decorations and let the paper dry, rather than use transparent tape. Customized wrapping, when prepared carefully, adds an unforgettable personal touch to gift giving.

GIFTS FROM THE KITCHEN AND THE GARDEN

'Tis the season to be giving! More than any other way, we make the spirit of Christmas come alive in the gifts we give. Avoid the malls this year by using this wide-ranging assortment of gift ideas from the kitchen and the garden to satisfy even the most hard-to-buy-for on your list.

Those tastes we all associate with Christmas—cinnamon, nutmeg, and cloves—are all there, and so are the their delicious aromas. Go ahead, give it a try! The key to a perfect gift is making it personal—and what could be more personal than a gift you've made yourself?

Although making these items will take some advance planning—starting weeks in advance to let fragrances or flavors mature, in some cases, or picking flowers or herbs for pressing or drying during the summer—the results will be a personalized gift that they'll know really comes from the heart. You may be able to find the specialty items needed to complete some of these projects locally—at a health food outlet or craft store, for example. Here are four personalized, homemade gifts that your friends, family, and colleagues will love!

Cranberry Scones

GIVE THESE ACCOMPANIED BY A SPECIAL JAR OF YOUR FAVORITE JAM OR JELLY.

1 cup sour cream
1½ teaspoon grated fresh orange peel
2 cups sifted all-purpose flour
½ cup granulated sugar
2 teaspoons baking powder
½ teaspoon salt
½ teaspoon baking soda
¼ cup butter or margarine, softened
1 large egg, at room temperature
¼ cup dried cranberries

WHY DOES *Santa* WEAR RED?

1. Preheat oven to 375 degrees Fahrenheit.

2. In a small bowl, combine sour cream and grated orange peel. Set aside.

3. In a large bowl, mix together the flour, granulated sugar, baking powder, and salt.

4. Using a pastry blender or 2 knives held together, cut in butter into the flour mixture until coarse crumbs form.

5. Break the egg in a small dish and beat well with a fork. Add the egg to the flour mixture and beat together until blended.

6. Add the sour cream and orange peel mixture and beat until just well blended.

7. Prepare a smooth surface (the kitchen counter is fine) by sprinkling it lightly with flour. Turn the dough out of the bowl. Using floured hands, knead the dough for about 30 seconds, or until smooth.

8. Taking only half the dough at a time, roll it out with a floured rolling pin until it is about half an inch thick. Using a 3-inch round cookie cutter, or similarly sized empty can, cut out rounds of dough.

9. Place the rounds 1 inch apart on a greased or nonstick cookie sheet. Before putting them in the oven, push 5 dried cranberries into the top of each one.

10. Bake until the tops are just barely browned, 12 to 18 minutes.

11. Let cool on wire racks. Makes 1 dozen scones.

Fruitcake Trio

CHRISTMAS WOULDN'T BE CHRISTMAS WITHOUT FRUITCAKE. THIS YEAR, SURPRISE YOUR FRIENDS BY GIVING THEM A FRUITCAKE YOU'VE PERSONALIZED TO THEIR OWN TASTE WITH THIS UNIQUE RECIPE.

Grease three 9″ × 5″ baking pans, then line with aluminum foil, then grease again. Now you're ready to prepare the main batter, after which you will follow the individualized instructions for making three quite different fruitcakes.

Main batter

1½ cup butter or margarine
1½ cup granulated sugar
1½ cup dark brown sugar, packed
9 large eggs
5 cups flour
1½ teaspoon each baking powder, salt, ground cinnamon,
   and ground nutmeg
1½ cup almonds, coarsely chopped

1.   In a large bowl, cream together butter and sugars.

2.   Beat in eggs at low speed, one at a time.

3. Slowly combine flour into butter mixture until it forms a light, fluffy batter.

4. In a small bowl, blend next four ingredients. Blend into batter.

5. By hand, fold in chopped almonds into the batter.

6. Preheat the oven to 300 degrees Fahrenheit.

At this point, divide batter into three different bowls to make the three different kinds of fruitcake. (You can choose to make three fruitcakes all of the same kind, but remember the amounts that follow are calculated for just one of each loaf.)

Dark Raisin Fruitcake

As directed above, take a third of the batter formed in the Main Batter section and add in the following until well blended:

¼ cup molasses
¼ teaspoon ground cloves
½ teaspoon ground allspice
2 cups each dark raisins and golden raisins
⅓ cups chopped dates

Morning Sunshine Fruitcake

As directed above, take a third of the batter formed in the Main Batter section and add in the following until well blended:

¼ cup orange juice
¼ teaspoon crushed cardamom seed
½ cup each candied orange and lemon peel
1 tablespoon lime juice
1½ cup mixed candied green cherries and candied yellow pineapple, chopped

Nut Lover's Fruitcake

As directed above, take a third of the batter formed in the Main Batter section and add in the following until well blended:

1 cup each pecans and walnuts, chopped
½ cup hazelnuts, chopped
1½ cup candied mixed fruit, chopped

1. Pour each batter into a prepared 9″ × 5″ pan.

2. Place a shallow pan of water on the lower oven rack to prevent drying.

3. Place the three filled pans next to each other on the top rack.

4. Cook for 1½ hours or until cake tester inserted into the center of each cake comes out clean. If the tops of the cakes start to become too brown near the end of cooking time, cover them with aluminum foil.

5. Cool in pans on cooling racks for 15 minutes. Using aluminum foil, carefully pull cakes out of pans and let cool on cooling racks.

If desired, wrap fruitcake in brandy-soaked cheesecloth and then in foil. Remoisten cloth every other week. Or wrap without liquor. Store for up to 2 months; freeze for longer periods. Before giving, glaze tops with small quantity of pineapple preserves, apple, jelly, or orange marmalade. Decorate with halved nuts and candied fruits.

Festive Pomanders

CLOVES, CINNAMON, ORANGES . . . THESE ARE SOME OF THE SCENTS THAT SAY, "IT'S CHRISTMASTIME." WHILE TRADITIONAL POMANDERS WERE ENTIRELY COVERED WITH CLOVES, COVERING THE ENTIRE FRUIT IS NOT NECESSARY FOR IMPRESSIVE RESULTS!

Fresh, unblemished citrus fruit, including oranges, lemons, limes
Fresh, unblemished apples
Approximately 1 ounce of whole cloves per pomander
3 tablespoons of each of the following per pomander: ground orris root, ground cinnamon, and ground allspice
Nut pick
Ribbons in various widths

1. Choose one fruit to start with (the pomanders will all be made the same way, but the apples are the easiest). Take a ribbon and run it around the fruit horizontally and then vertically. Hold together at the top with a straight pin or two.

2. Take a ribbon of another width (either wider or narrower) and wrap it once around the fruit, halving one of the "sections" made with the first ribbon.

3. Insert the cloves into the fruit, only in the areas not covered by the ribbon.

4. Take the ribbon off the fruit and set aside.

5. In a small bowl combine the powdered orris root, cinnamon, and ground allspice. Mix well to combine.

6. Put the piece of fruit in the bowl, pushing it gently into the spice mix. With a spoon, spoon the mixture over the fruit until it is covered.

7. Set aside in a dry, dark place for at least 3–4 weeks, spooning the mixture over the fruit and rotating the fruit every few days.

8. When the fruit is dried completely, it will have shrunk to be somewhat smaller than its original size. Put the ribbons back in the original spaces made for them on the fruit. Fasten with hot glue on the top. Tie another ribbon around the dried fruit, this time with a loop at the top for hanging. Add dried flowers and a bow, using a glue gun.

Pineapples are preserved in the same way as oranges and apples, but because of their size, they need to be begun in June to have sufficient time to dry out by December. Place the cloves along the diamond pattern in the skin. Tie a ribbon under the leaves of the plant when it's all dried out, and you have an excellent tropical pomander.

Fragrant Herbal Tree

CUSHION THIS SCENT-SATIONAL CENTERPIECE IN A LARGE GILT GIFT BOX AMID ALTERNATING LAYERS OF RED, WHITE, AND GREEN TISSUE PAPER SCATTERED WITH TINY GOLD STAR SEQUINS. IT'S A PERFECT GIFT FOR A HOUSEGUEST TO GIVE TO HIS OR HER HOSTESS.

1 Styrofoam cone (12" × 4⅞")
Gold spray paint
2 to 3 cups mixed floral all-natural potpourri (not the kind containing scented wood shavings)
9-inch length 4-inch-wide red paper twist
10-inch length ⅛-inch-wide gold ribbon
Approximately 100 individual florets of dried white statice, or a similar flower
16-inch length 1-inch wide ruffled lace
One spool of thread, any color
Equipment needed: mini kitchen chopper, 1-inch wide foam brush, scissors, floral sealant or unscented hairspray, straight pin, cotton swabs, craft glue, glue gun, and glue sticks

1. Spray-paint the Styrofoam cone gold. Let dry.

2. Using a glue gun, glue the lace on the bottom of the cone, so most of it is showing when the cone is set on a table. Set aside.

3. Look over your potpourri and discard (or save for other usage) any hard seeds or floral heads that your kitchen chopper won't be able to chop.

4. Use your mini chopper to pulverize about ½ cup of potpourri at a time. Pulsing the cutting blades, reduce the larger pieces of the potpourri to quarter-inch fragments. Reserve the prepared potpourri in a medium mixing bowl, until you have approximately 1 cup of material. Prepare additional quantities as needed.

5. Put a small puddle of craft glue on a small foam plate and mix with a little water to make it more spreadable, but not so it loses its tackiness.

6. Using a foam brush, "paint" the top half of one side of the foam cone with glue.

7. Working quickly, press the potpourri into the glue, making sure to cover as much of the cone as possible. Begin another section.

8. When you've covered the entire cone (except for the bottom), look it over and touch up any bald spots, using cotton swabs dipped in glue to put a dab of glue on the spot and press in enough potpourri to cover. Spray potpourri-covered cone lightly with a floral fixative or unscented hairspray to set loose petals.

9. Attach a piece of thread to the top of the cone using a pin, and drape it in a spiral pattern around the tree (much like draping a garland on a Christmas tree). Follow the string as a pattern for placement of the dried statice florets.

10. Using a glue gun, glue the florets in a line following a spiral pattern from the top to the bottom of the cone and once around the top and base of the cone. Work from top to bottom so florets have their blooms facing at an upward angle and so that each dried flower covers the bottom of the stem of the bloom preceding it. Discard the string and the pin. Lightly spray a second coat of the floral fixative on the cone to cover the statice.

11. Flatten out the piece of paper twist, fold it in half, and cut a V-shape out of each end, with the point pointing in. Unfold.

12. Glue the gold ribbon down the middle of the paper twist, turning the ends around to the backside of the twist.

13. Tie a knot in the middle of the paper twist, fluffing it out and shaping it to perch on the top of the cone. Use glue gun to attach it to the top of the cone.

14. To revive the scent of the potpourri, place several drops of potpourri oil at several locations on the tree, if desired.

"The Holly and the Ivy":
A Present Left by the Peasantry

"The Holly and the Ivy," traditional British song

The holly and the ivy,
When they are both full grown,
Of all the trees that are in the wood
The holly bears the crown.

Refrain: O the rising of the sun,
And the running of the deer,
The playing of the merry organ,
Sweet singing in the choir.

The holly bears a blossom,
As white as the lily flower,
And Mary bore sweet Jesus Christ
To be our sweet Saviour.
(Refrain)

The holly bears a berry,
As red as any blood,

And Mary bore sweet Jesus Christ
To do poor sinners good.
(Refrain)

The holly bears a prickle,
As sharp as any thorn,
And Mary bore sweet Jesus Christ
On Christmas Day in the morn.
(Refrain)

The holly bears a bark,
As bitter as any gall,
And Mary bore sweet Jesus Christ
For to redeem us all.
(Refrain)

The holly and the ivy,
When they are both full grown,
Of all the trees that are in the wood
The holly bears the crown.
(Refrain)

"The Holly and the Ivy" is a traditional British Christmas carol. It was composed in the 1700s in western England's Gloucestershire region. The music is from an old French carol, and the lyrics are typical of the English folksong tradition. Like so much of the old folk music that has emerged from the common people or peasantry of a country, this music's authorship is unknown.

Note: In English lore, holly and ivy were often personified as male and female, which made them popular topics for carols. In the words to this carol, however, the holly represents the Virgin Mary, while the berry stands for the infant Jesus.

giving and receiving

*T*he most obvious feature of the modern American Christmas is the giving and receiving of gifts. Gifts have become almost synonymous with December 25, so much so that some fear they have overshadowed the true meaning of the holiday. What follows is a brief history of the Christmas giving tradition. If you still can't think of something to get for someone special, the following pages may surprise and/or inspire you!

WHY DOES *Santa* WEAR RED?

GIFTS AND CELEBRATIONS, OLD AND NEW In ancient Rome, gifts were exchanged during the Saturnalia and the New Year's celebrations. At first these gifts were very simple—a few twigs from a sacred grove, statues of gods, food, and the like. Many gifts were in the form of vegetation in honor of Strenia, goddess of the New Year. During the Northern European Yule, fertility was celebrated with gifts made of wheat products, such as bread and alcohol.

As time went on, gifts became more elaborate and less edible. While most of this giving was done on a voluntary basis, history has had its share of leaders who did their level best to ensure they'd have plenty of gifts to open. One year Emperor Caligula of Rome declared to all that he would be receiving presents on New Year's Day; gifts he deemed inadequate or inappropriate were ridiculed. (As readers of Robert Graves's works will remember, displeasing Caligula could be a dangerous undertaking.) Then there was Henry III, who closed down the merchants of England one December because he was not impressed with the amount of their monetary gifts.

✸ Looking Back ✸

Ho, ho, ho: If you'd been a merchant whose cash gift for the ruler was too small to suit England's King Henry III, you might have found yourself out of business.

Although we may question his Christmas spirit, Henry was only following long-established tradition in focusing on end-of-way gifts. Like many old customs, gift exchange was difficult to get rid of even as Christianity spread and gained official status. Early church leaders tried to outlaw the custom, but the people cherished it too much to let it go. So instead, as was beginning to be the pattern, church leaders sought a Christian justification for the practice. The justification was found in the Magi's act of bearing gifts to the infant Jesus, and in the concept that Christ was a gift from God to the world, bringing in turn the gift of redemption and everlasting life.

After Christianity had established itself throughout Europe, Christmas celebrations were quite common; gift giving as a component of Christmas Day, however, was not. The concept of a gift exchange on the holiday itself remained more the exception than the rule, and much of the gift giving at that time was confined to New Year's, as in the days of the ancient Romans. Some countries, particularly those under Spanish cultural influence, saved gift giving for Epiphany (January 6), the day marking the visit of the Magi to Jesus.

TODAY'S SPENDING BUDGET What is the price you would pay for all twelve items in "The Twelve Day's of Christmas?" Have you ever considered what it would cost to buy a pear tree? And why five gold rings? Why not just one? According to the study, put out every year, by PNC Wealth Management, the tab was a small fortune in 2006! Check it out below.

- *Partridge:* $15.00
- *Pear tree:* $129.00
- *Two turtledoves:* $40.00

WHY DOES *Santa* WEAR RED?

- *Three French hens:* $45.00
- *Four calling birds:* $479.96
- *Five gold rings:* $325.00
- *Six geese-a-laying:* $300.00
- *Seven swans-a-swimming:* $4,200.00
- *Eight maids-a-milking:* $41.20
- *Nine ladies dancing:* $4,759.19
- *Ten lords-a-leaping:* $4,160.25
- *Eleven pipers piping:* $2,124.00
- *Twelve drummers drumming:* $2,301.00
- *Total Christmas price index:* $18,919.60

THE ART (AND COST) OF GIVING Back in ancient Roman times, a citizen might have received the makings of a nice salad for Saturnalia; a Victorian chap, on the other hand, might have the pleasure of a new pipe or a snuff box. But what about the United States, the country that put the "C" (for commercialism) in Christmas giving and receiving? What gifts were the most popular over the years, as the giving tradition unfolded?

In the first part of the twentieth century, gifts were a great deal simpler than they are today. Clothing was a staple for adults and children, with the latter getting a toy or two for enjoyment. The first decade of the twentieth century gave us two childhood classics: the crayon and the teddy bear.

During this time, the crayon and the teddy bear took their place among children's classic toys also.

Despite the Depression of the 1930s, toy manufacturers continued to come up with occasional classics that people somehow managed to scrape enough money together to buy. Yo-yos were quite popular. Those who have seen *A Christmas Story*, a delightful 1983 movie about one boy's Christmas wish during this era, will doubtless recall the Red Ryder BB gun, a big seller in real life. The gun got its name from a comic book character, one of the first of a very long (and ever-growing) list of toys based on comic, television, or movie characters. Howdy Doody, for instance, was as popular in his day as Bart Simpson is to today's kids.

After America made it through the Depression and World War II, the country began to prosper as never before. Industry and technology went into in high gear; more and better jobs meant Americans had more discretionary income to spend on things like Christmas gifts. It was the beginning of a glorious time for toys, technology, and treats for all ages to enjoy!

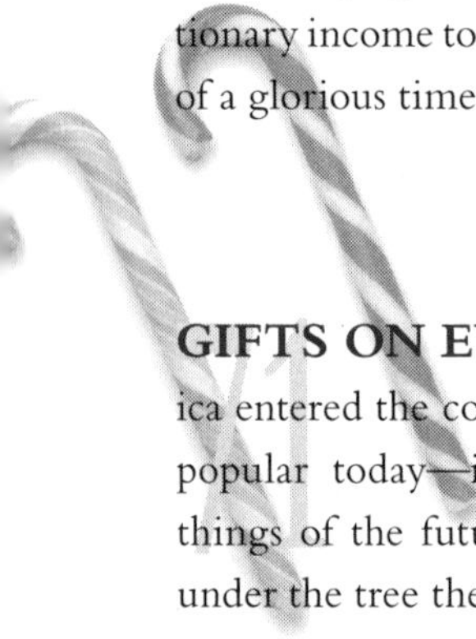

GIFTS ON EVERYONE'S LIST Two decades ago, when America entered the consumer electronics age in earnest, the gifts that are most popular today—including iPods, PlayStations, and Xboxes—were still things of the future. The toys and electronics that Santa is asked to put under the tree these days hadn't even been created back in the 1980s.

Today's kids are so savvy about electronics that ten-year-olds already have profiles and pictures on *Myspace.com*, know how to find products they want on the Internet, and understand how to manipulate computers, digital cameras, and other electronic devices better than the generation before them. They know how to find the Harry Potter Web sites for kids, play interactive games with their friends, and do brainteasers on the computer.

For twenty-first-century kids, the computer is both a toy and a tool. They can use it to do schoolwork or to chat with friends a continent away. This means Santa has to learn some new technical terms.

If we want to consider how we got to this point, let's look back on the toys that shaped the Christmases of past decades. During the 1980s, Cabbage Patch Kids, video games, and everything Teenage Mutant Ninja Turtles were hot. Other popular toys from the decade of the 1980s included the talking Pee-Wee Herman doll, assorted Smurf paraphernalia, the Li'l Miss Makeup doll, and, for younger kids, the Fisher-Price tape recorder. For adults, top gifts of the era included exercise bikes, ice cream makers, Trivial Pursuit games, Pictionary games, camcorders, VCRs, and, toward the end of the decade, laptop computers.

As the 1990s began, yet another television-spawned merchandising bonanza enjoyed remarkable popularity, but this time the innocence of Howdy Doody was nowhere to be found. Bart Simpson, who would probably have done something quite rude to Howdy on principle if he had gotten within a yard of him, became one of the biggest television stars in the country. Bart and his demented, anti-utopian world, complete with odd relatives, served as a weekly vehicle for biting social satire and remarks likely to embarrass teachers when repeated in class. Kids couldn't get enough of him, and cash registers rang up huge sales for his books, clothes, and other products during the holidays.

The 1980s success of high-tech toys carried over into the 1990s. Yet ironically, and despite white-hot sales of things like Power Rangers sets, the toys that have remained popular through decades of trends are the ones that don't require batteries, plugs, headphones, or television tie-ins—just imagination, the desire for fun, and maybe a few friends. The chances are good that children will, for the foreseeable future, wake up Christmas morning and find that Santa has left them one or two things just like those that he left for their parents many years ago. And as we head into the next century, dolls, board games, building blocks, stuffed animals, Play Doh, Legos, toy guns, crayons, and bicycles are sure to make that journey, too.

TOYS AND THE BABY-BOOMER GENERATION

Toys made their mark (in the consumer industry) at a very specific time in America's history. The number of American children exploded in the years after World War II, and so, not surprisingly, did the national appetite for toys. Some of the most enduring playthings of today—such as the Etch-A-Sketch, Play Doh modeling clay, and the Barbie doll—were introduced in the decade and a half following the end of World War II.

What did the initial wave of baby boomers want for Christmas? The list from the decade of the 1950s includes things like these:

WHY DOES *Santa* WEAR RED?

- Howdy Doody toys
- Jackie Robinson toy
- The Red Ryder No. 960 Noisemaker BB Gun
- Silly Putty
- Barbie dolls
- G.I. Joes
- Frisbees (originally called Pluto Platters)
- Hula hoops
- Mr. Potato Head sets
- Betsy Wetsy dolls
- Lego blocks
- The Game of Life
- Pogo sticks
- Matchbox cars

❧ Festive Fact ❧

The good people at Mattel, who keep track of such things, report that more Barbie dolls have been manufactured since her introduction than there have been people born in the United States during the same period.

By the middle 1960s, the American middle class, against which many young people had begun to rebel, was buying for Christmas at a fevered pitch—and children weren't the only ones on the receiving end. Adults were indulging in some "toys" of their own, and not all of them were cheap. There were home steam baths and saunas, jewelry, and, for quiet (or not-so-quiet) evenings at home, newfangled color television sets. As one Chicago retailer put it, Americans were "loaded."

And it seems that some retailers priced their merchandise based on that belief. For one Christmas buying season, Tiffany's in New York offered their upscale patrons the opportunity to purchase a $550 sterling-silver watering can. Neiman-Marcus's offerings ranged from $300 lace hankies to $10,000 wristwatches to $20,000 teapots to $125,000 diamond rings. Not to be outdone, San Francisco's Joseph Magnin sold three-liter flacons of Shalimar perfume for $2,500, to be delivered to the lucky recipient via Rolls-Royce. Other popular 1960s Christmas gifts included things like these:

- Everything Beatles: records, coloring books, toy guitars, lunchboxes, and related merchandise
- Hot Wheels miniature cars
- The Super Ball
- Instant Insanity, a colored cube game akin to the later Rubik's Cube
- Tonka trucks
- Twister ("Right foot green!")

Board games were also a very popular gift category. Strong sellers from the decade include Clue, Risk, Candyland, Go to the Head of the Class, Cooties, Scrabble, Yahtzee, Operation!, Parcheesi, and Jeopardy (the Art Fleming, rather than Alex Trebek, incarnation). The Mousetrap game sold 1.2 million copies in 1963. During the early years of the baby boom, toys for kids and adults became more popular than ever!

CHRISTMAS BUSINESS EMERGES By the late nineteenth century, the simple and essentially non-materialistic gift giving tradition had begun to wither away. Christmas had come face to face with commercialism, and the new message was simple: Buy!

It wasn't long before shopping and the idea of gifts had woven itself into the fabric of Christmas. This transition was encouraged by merchants (and everyone else in the developing economies of Europe and America) who stood to benefit from a year-end buying binge. It was—and is—an open question whether this development did more harm than good to the holiday. Skeptics wonder whether the emphasis on buying, shopping, and getting ultimately brings more happiness or disappointment—especially to those who can afford little. Others have found a new and robust variation on the holiday spirit in the shopping-related hustle and bustle around Christmastime. Perhaps, they argue, it is too much to expect that Christmas, having adapted itself to so many civilizations over the years, wouldn't be affected by the modern consumer culture in which we live.

In the end, it's likely that the best way to approach Christmas gift giving is with both viewpoints in mind. Most parents of young children are unwilling or unable to mount the sustained battle necessary to do away entirely with what might be called the "gimme" Christmas—but there's no reason some of the laudable spirit of past holidays can't be incorporated as well.

What Is Figgy Pudding, Anyway?: "We Wish You a Merry Christmas"

"WE WISH YOU A MERRY CHRISTMAS," TRADITIONAL BRITISH SONG

We wish you a Merry Christmas,
We wish you a Merry Christmas,
We wish you a Merry Christmas
And a Happy New Year!
Glad tidings we bring,
To you and your kin
We wish you a Merry Christmas
And a Happy New Year!

Although this traditional carol can be traced back to sixteenth-century England, the author of the work is unknown. The song's lyrics refer to carolers singing for wealthy people and being offered treats, among them figgy pudding, a dish in which figs are the main ingredient. This particular pudding has fallen out of food fashion in England, but remains somewhat similar to other traditional Christmas puddings. Besides figs, the pudding contained eggs, milk, sugar, lemon and orange peel, nuts, rum, and spices such as cinnamon, ginger, and cloves.

a pop-culture christmas

When we think of Christmas these days, we often think of television, music, and the movies. The Grinch, George Bailey, Rudolph the Red-Nosed Reindeer, and a host of other figures who came to prominence after World War II now play an important part in our celebration of the holiday. The popularity of these figures is fundamentally different than the popularity enjoyed by, say, a classic Christmas carol. We learned about these characters not over centuries, but suddenly, and with bewildering speed, thanks to modern means of communication.

Rather than pretend that the mass media aspect of Christmas is somehow heretical, it's far preferable to think of it as a lot of fun—and it is celebrated here. Dig in!

THE ULTIMATE CHRISTMAS QUIZ: ARE YOU UP ON YOUR TINSEL TRIVIA? Test your Christmas prowess with this comprehensive quiz: songs, films, television programs, and videos. Looking back as far as the 1930s to today, how much do you really know about Christmas trivia? Grab a separate sheet of paper and jot down your answers. (Note: This is a particularly good group activity for a Christmas party!)

1. Which band recorded "Walking in a Winter Wonderland" but was famous for "Here Comes the Rain Again"?

   (a) Beatles

   (b) Toto

   (c) America

   (d) The Eurythmics

2. What is it that the little girl wants for Christmas in the 1991 film *All I Want for Christmas*?

   (a) Her two front teeth

   (b) A life-size poster of Keanu Reeves

   (c) For her divorced parents to get back together

   (d) An end to the blood feud that has set her town against itself for seven years

3. Which *Lethal Weapon* movie opened with "Jingle Bell Rock"?

    (a) The first

    (b) The second

    (c) The third

    (d) The fourth

4. In the movie *A Christmas Story*, why is the boy's mother afraid to let him have a BB gun?

    (a) She's afraid he'll forget all about his other Christmas toys.

    (b) She's afraid he'll shoot his eye out.

    (c) She's afraid he'll run away from home, secure in his newfound power.

    (d) She's afraid he'll have an accident while cleaning the gun.

5. How did *Amahl and the Night Visitors* come to be written?

    (a) It was composed by a medieval monk who left the score behind a stone wall in a monastery, where it would rest undisturbed for two and a half centuries.

    (b) It was written at the request of His Royal Highness King Edward II.

    (c) It was commissioned for a special Christmas television broadcast.

    (d) It was composed for the London stage in the early 1930s.

6. Who plays Bob Cratchit in 1992's *The Muppet Christmas Carol*?

    (a) Michael Caine

    (b) John Denver

    (c) Bob Denver

    (d) Kermit the Frog

7. Charles Dickens himself makes an appearance in *The Muppet Christmas Carol*. Who plays him?

    (a) Hunter S. Thompson

    (b) Michael J. Fox

    (c) George C. Scott

    (d) The Great Gonzo

8. In the 1949 classic *Holiday Affair*, what two actors played suitors to Janet Leigh?

    (a) Robert Mitchum and Wendell Corey

    (b) Dean Martin and Jerry Lewis

    (c) Bud Abbott and Lou Costello

    (d) Bob Hope and Bing Crosby

9. Why does Ernest want to find a replacement for Santa in 1988's *Ernest Saves Christmas*?

    (a) Ernest has it on good authority that Santa's best days are behind him, although the old man refuses to face it.

    (b) Santa has decided that it's time to retire.

    (c) The reindeer won't work on Christmas Eve anymore because Santa refuses to pay them time and a half.

    (d) Santa is missing.

10. In the movie *The Santa Clause*, Tim Allen's character accidentally kills whom?

    (a) A neighbor

    (b) An elf

    (c) Rudolph

    (d) Santa

11. For which of the following films did Irving Berlin compose the song "White Christmas?"

    (a) *White Christmas*

    (b) *Holiday Inn*

    (c) *It's a Wonderful Life*

    (d) *Last Tango in Paris*

12. What is the request made to Heaven by a recently dead police officer (played by Mickey Rooney) in 1984's *It Came Upon a Midnight Clear*?

    (a) That he be allowed to put on one last show in the barn.

    (b) That peace on earth and goodwill among men be made manifest.

    (c) That Santa be allowed to make his annual trip despite the evil designs of the Anti-Christmas League.

    (d) That he be allowed to spend one final Christmas with his grandson.

13. Who played the hapless slogan composer in 1940's *Christmas in July*?

    (a) Ronald Reagan

    (b) Jimmy Stewart

(c) Preston Sturges

(d) Dick Powell

14. Of the following, which was a slogan that was actually used in *Christmas in July*?

(a) "If you can't sleep, it's not the coffee, it must be the bunk."

(b) "Make it a special Christmas. Make it a regular Christmas. Chew Simulax tablets."

(c) "Coffee the way it was meant to be."

(d) "Good to the last drop."

15. In what year was *A Charlie Brown Christmas* first broadcast?

(a) 1963

(b) 1964

(c) 1965

(d) 1966

16. In the 1954 movie *White Christmas*, why was the old New England inn in such desperate financial straits?

(a) The previous owner had been subject to a lawsuit, but had concealed this fact from prospective buyers.

(b) The town suffered a major blow when a local shoe factory closed.

(c) The inn was a ski resort, and there hadn't been any snow for a year.

(d) The tourist guides had their doubts about the kitchen help.

17. In the 1996 movie *Jingle All the Way*, what famous actor starred as Howard Langston and in real life pursued a career in politics?

    (a) Harrison Ford

    (b) Leonardo DiCaprio

    (c) Ralph Fiennes

    (d) Arnold Schwarzenegger

18. What's the name of the character Bing Crosby plays in *Holiday Inn*?

    (a) Winston Smith

    (b) Jim Hardy

    (c) Charles Foster Kane

    (d) Mike Cleary

19. Why was Macaulay Culkin exiled to his room in 1990's *Home Alone?*

    (a) He set an elaborate trap in his smug older brother's room.

    (b) He was discovered attempting to tape his weird uncle while he, the uncle, was taking a shower.

    (c) He had been watching too many old movies on video.

    (d) He was being punished for a disastrous kitchen spill.

20. Name the two bad guys in the *Home Alone* movies who eventually became famous as the "Wet Bandits."

    (a) Joe and Ratso

    (b) Harry and Mary

    (c) Harry and Tonto

    (d) Melvin and Howard

21. In the first *Home Alone* movie, where was the family headed for Christmas?

    (a) Paris

    (b) Barcelona

    (c) Florida

    (d) San Juan

22. How is Joe Pesci disguised as he scopes out the neighborhood in the early scenes of the first *Home Alone* movie?

    (a) As a mobster

    (b) As a policeman

    (c) As a mailman

    (d) As an exterminator

23. In the first *Home Alone* movie, why did Macaulay Culkin head-butt his older brother in the stomach?

    (a) The brother wouldn't let him have a turn with the Nintendo game.

    (b) The brother took the last of the cheese pizza.

    (c) The brother was threatening to squeal about a bad grade on a spelling test.

    (d) The brother was choking on something.

24. What is the name of Macaulay Culkin's character in the *Home Alone* movies?

    (a) Kevin McAllister

    (b) Kevin McReynolds

    (c) Kevin MacArthur

    (d) Kevin McCall

25. What is the name of the scary old guy in the first *Home Alone* movie?

    (a) Cratchit

    (b) Bob

    (c) Marley

    (d) Marlon

26. Whom does Macaulay Culkin approach and ask for the return of his family in the first *Home Alone* movie?

    (a) The pigeon lady

    (b) Santa Claus

    (c) A hotel employee

    (d) A policeman

27. In *Home Alone II*, where was the family headed for Christmas?

    (a) Paris

    (b) Barcelona

    (c) Florida

    (d) San Juan

28. Which of the following occurs in *Home Alone II*?

    (a) Joe Pesci's hair is set on fire.

    (b) A rope Joe Pesci is climbing is doused with kerosene and set on fire.

    (c) Joe Pesci is struck in the head by a huge lead pipe.

    (d) All of the above.

29. What is the first image after the opening credits in Frank Capra's 1946 classic *It's a Wonderful Life*?

(a) A sky full of stars, three of which blink as a number of angels speak.

(b) George Bailey sledding down a hill on a snow shovel.

(c) George's younger brother Harry Bailey sledding down a hill on a snow shovel.

(d) A sign reading "You Are Now in Bedford Falls."

30. What is the name of the angel who is assigned the task of saving George Bailey's life in *It's a Wonderful Life*?

(a) Lumen Phosphor

(b) Fluor Candle

(c) Clarence Oddbody

(d) Tom Sawyer

31. In the song "Santa Baby," who wants a sable, a convertible, a yacht, the deed to a platinum mine, a duplex, decorations from Tiffany's, and a ring from Santa Baby?

(a) Beyonce

(b) Cher

(c) Madonna

(d) Britney Spears

32. Had George Bailey, the main character in *It's a Wonderful Life,* never been born, what would Bedford Falls have been called?

    (a) Morgantown

    (b) Pottersville

    (c) Gowerville

    (d) Robinwood

33. In *It's a Wonderful Life,* why was young George Bailey hit by his boss?

    (a) He was late for work.

    (b) He'd been neglecting his duties, paying too much attention to the girls at the soda counter.

    (c) He hadn't delivered a prescription as he'd been ordered to do.

    (d) He kept daydreaming about traveling to foreign lands.

34. What are the names of the policeman and the taxi driver in *It's a Wonderful Life*?

    (a) Bert and Ernie

    (b) Tom and Jerry

    (c) Mike and Terry

    (d) Billy and Rick

35. Which of the following A-level Hollywood scriptwriters toiled on early drafts of *It's a Wonderful Life,* only to have his work rejected?

    (a) Dalton Trumbo

    (b) Marc Connelley

(c) Clifford Odets

(d) All of the above

36. In *It's a Wonderful Life*, what is the nickname of the little girl whose flower petals wind up in George Bailey's pocket on the night he considers killing himself?

(a) Daisy

(b) Zuzu

(c) Pitter-Pat

(d) Bunkadoodle

37. What, according to a child in the Bailey family, does it mean when you hear bells ringing?

(a) You've been knocked out.

(b) You've just won the final round of *Jeopardy.*

(c) You have tinnitus.

(d) An angel has just gotten his wings.

38. Who played the lead role in *It Happened One Christmas*, the 1977 television remake of *It's a Wonderful Life*?

(a) Henry Winkler

(b) Marlo Thomas

(c) Jimmy Stewart

(d) John Denver

39. What does Lucy want for Christmas in *A Charlie Brown Christmas*?
    (a) Real estate
    (b) A pair of ice skates
    (c) A trip to Disneyland
    (d) A new friend

40. Name the Mafioso movie that premiered on December 25, 1990.
    (a) *Prizzi's Honor*
    (b) *Godfather III*
    (c) *Goodfellas*
    (d) *Donnie Brasco*

41. How did Edmund Gwenn (in the role of Kris Kringle in *Miracle on 34th Street*) come to the notice of the management at Macy's?
    (a) He answered an advertisement for department store Santas.
    (b) He saw that the Santa in the store's holiday float was so drunk that he couldn't stand up, and volunteered to replace him.
    (c) He started handing out presents to children in the store.
    (d) He showed up at the personnel office dressed in a Santa Claus costume.

42. Name the child star whose career was launched by her appearance in *Miracle on 34th Street*.
    (a) Shirley Temple
    (b) Elizabeth Taylor
    (c) Judy Garland
    (d) Natalie Wood

WHY DOES *Santa* WEAR RED?

43. When was *Miracle on 34th Street* first released in movie theaters?

   (a) The late autumn of 1947

   (b) The winter of 1948

   (c) The late autumn of 1948

   (d) The summer of 1947

44. In *Miracle on 34th Street*, whom did Edmund Gwenn list as "next of kin" on his Macy's employment application form?

   (a) His invaluable colleague Anna Botelho

   (b) Clarence Oddbody

   (c) The children of the world

   (d) Reindeer

45. In *Miracle on 34th Street*, what precipitated Edmund Gwenn's being committed to Bellevue?

   (a) He declared that he was not Santa after all, but rather the Tooth Fairy.

   (b) He struck a psychiatrist on the head with a cane.

   (c) He wandered the streets of New York without apparent purpose.

   (d) He failed a polygraph test administered by the New York City Police Department.

46. Who played the cat burglar who took a family hostage in the 1994 movie *The Ref*?

   (a) Denis Leary

   (b) Joe Pesci

(c) Kevin Spacey

(d) Brad Pitt

47. Who plays Marley's ghost in Scrooge, the 1970 adaptation of *A Christmas Carol*?

    (a) John Gielgud

    (b) Alex Guinness

    (c) Jason Robards

    (d) Martin Sheen

48. What did *Frosty the Snowman* put on that made him come alive?

    (a) An overcoat

    (b) Mittens

    (c) Boots

    (d) Magical hat

49. Red Skelton and Vincent Price teamed up in a classic restaurant sketch in the hour-long Christmas special *Red Skelton's Christmas Dinner*. What were the names of the characters they played?

    (a) Max and Dan

    (b) Freddy the Freeloader and Professor Humperdue

    (c) Dracula and Dr. Frankenstein

    (d) Bud and Lou

50. Who are Santa's incompetent assistants in the 1934 film *Babes in Toyland*?

    (a) Charlie Chaplin and Buster Keaton

    (b) W. C. Fields and Mae West

    (c) Groucho, Chico, and Harpo Marx

    (d) Stan Laurel and Oliver Hardy

ANSWERS

1.	d		18.	b
2.	c		19.	d
3.	a		20.	b
4.	b		21.	a
5.	c		22.	b
6.	d		23.	b
7.	d		24.	a
8.	a		25.	c
9.	b		26.	b
10.	d		27.	c
11.	b		28.	d
12.	d		29.	d
13.	d		30.	c
14.	a		31.	c
15.	c		32.	b
16.	c		33.	c
17.	d		34.	a

35.	d		43.	d
36.	b		44.	d
37.	d		45.	b
38.	b		46.	a
39.	a		47.	b
40.	b		48.	d
41.	b		49.	b
42.	d		50.	d

HOW DO YOU OR YOUR GROUP RATE?

🎵 **0 to 10 correct:** As a general rule, you've been doing something other than watching television at Christmas time over the past thirty or forty years. But maybe you got the easy ones. You've been rocking to "Jingle Bell Rock," but you could probably stand to rent *It's a Wonderful Life* a time or two.

🎵 **11 to 20 correct:** You've definitely got the holiday spirit, but Andy Williams still thinks you can do better.

🎵 **21 to 30 correct:** Nice work. You can probably recite the lyrics to "White Christmas" without batting an eye. Spread the good cheer!

🎵 **31 to 40 correct:** Ho, ho ho! Somewhere in heaven, Nat King Cole is crooning "The Christmas Song" just for you.

🎵 **41 to 50 correct:** You can probably recite the entire script of *The Grinch Who Stole Christmas* verbatim—from deep sleep. Take a bow.

TOP TWENTY MOVIES THAT MAKE US MERRY

Looking for something good to watch on DVD? Holiday movies are often hard to track down in December, but if you use this checklist you'll always have something good to ask for when the clerk says, "Sorry, that's out right now."

The vast majority of these movies are suitable for viewing by all members of the family. Still, exceptions may be found on any list, so look at the ratings before sharing with your kids.

How many of the following have you seen?

❒ *A Charlie Brown Christmas*
❒ *A Christmas Carol* (1938 version)
❒ *A Christmas Carol* (1951 version)
❒ *A Christmas Story*
❒ *A Christmas to Remember*
❒ *Frosty the Snowman*
❒ *How the Grinch Stole Christmas*
❒ *Home Alone and Home Alone II*
❒ *It's a Wonderful Life*
❒ *Elf*
❒ *Miracle on 34th Street* (1947 version)

❒ *Miracle on 34th Street* (1994 version)
❒ *National Lampoon's Christmas Vacation* (1)
❒ *National Lampoon's Christmas Vacation* (2)
❒ *The Nutcracker*
❒ *Home Alone*
❒ *Love Actually*
❒ *The Ten Commandments*
❒ *White Christmas*
❒ *Ernest Saves Christmas*

IT'S A WONDERFUL MOVIE If you asked twenty people to name their top-ten Christmas films of all time, odds are that nineteen of them would find a place on the list for Frank Capra's 1946 Christmas classic, *It's a Wonderful Life*. But how well did the picture do in its initial release?

During World War II, Capra, who had scored with such hits as *It Happened One Night*, *Mr. Smith Goes to Washington*, and *Mr. Deeds Goes to Town*, headed the government's Office of War Information, and directed the powerful *Why We Fight* series of documentaries.

When the war ended, Capra returned to Hollywood and, with William Wyler, George Stevens, and Samuel Briskin, formed Liberty Pictures—an independent production company in an era of big-studio moviemaking. For his first project, he bought the rights to a short piece by Philip Van Doren Stern called "The Greatest Gift." It told the tale of a man who was afforded the opportunity to see what life would have been like if he had never been born.

Capra asked Jimmy Stewart, who had returned from active duty as an air force pilot, to be his leading man. To win Stewart's commitment before any script existed, Capra had to give a verbal summary of the plot he had in mind. According to Stewart, the account was a rambling one that had to do with an angel who didn't have any wings yet, a good man named George Bailey who wanted to see the world but never got to, a savings and loan company, a small town, and a misplaced wad of money—among many, many other things. Although Capra's summary left Stewart more baffled than ever about what the film was actually about, he agreed to do the picture. Donna Reed, Lionel Barrymore, and Thomas Mitchell also signed on.

The picture was filmed over the summer of 1946. All the snow in the winter scenes is fake; all the actors in overcoats and mittens were sweltering. When the movie was released in late December of 1946, it received generally positive critical notices, but it flopped at the box office. There are a number of theories as to exactly why this occurred.

Whether it was because of the tone of the film, the competitive pressures from the big studios, the timing, or a combination of all three, *It's a Wonderful Life* was anything but a wonderful experience for the fledgling Liberty Films studio.

By the end of the year, that project and others like it had brought the company into serious financial trouble. To avoid personal responsibility for Liberty's debts, Capra and his partners dissolved the studio—and, in so doing, paved the way for the remarkable revival of the story of George Bailey of Bedford Falls.

The irony is that if Liberty had not failed, *It's a Wonderful Life* might never have become a holiday tradition. Television, not the movies, was the medium by which Capra's film became widely known and loved. This was largely because the copyright to the film fell into the public domain at a time when broadcasters were hungry for cheap holiday-oriented programming. If you had a copy of the film, you could show it, period. You could also delete as many scenes from it as you pleased in order to accommodate television's insatiable appetite for commercial breaks, a fact that has infuriated many a Capra purist.

Thankfully, the unedited version of the film is available on videotape. (Turner Entertainment, which obtained the RKO library, has the original negative).

Whoops! Film Flubs in Capra's Holiday Masterpiece

In the dinner scene before the big dance, when Harry Bailey says, "Annie, my sweet, have you got those pies?" the water-pitcher on the table is about one-third full. Later in the scene, without anyone's assistance, the level has mysteriously risen to about one-half.

Shortly after Mary loses her bathrobe and dashes into a nearby bush, she tells George that she's hiding in the hydrangea bush. It's hard to tell what the set designer was getting at with this "plant," but one thing's for certain: It ain't no hydrangea bush. (Then again, perhaps the stress of the moment has gotten to Mary!)

Watch very closely after George tosses the robe onto the bush; the robe vanishes in the next shot!

Right before George's bitter line "I wish I'd never been born," Clarence Oddbody is standing with his arms at his side. But in the very next shot, Clarence's arms are crossed.

Near the end of the long final scene of the film, Zuzu reaches for the pocket watch before the stocky man pulls it out of her coat to surprise her with it.

WHAT WE WATCHED ON CHRISTMAS EVE—
25 YEARS OF HOLIDAY VIEWING

CHRISTMAS EVE, 1970

The Flip Wilson Show
Boughs of Holly
Story Theater

CHRISTMAS EVE, 1971

J.T.
The Odd Couple
Beethoven's Birthday

CHRISTMAS EVE, 1972

Christmas with the King Family
The Miracles of Christmas
The Wonderful World of Disney

CHRISTMAS EVE, 1973

Gunsmoke
*An American Christmas in Words
    and Music*
A Dream of Christmas

CHRISTMAS EVE, 1974

Holy Year Jubilee
Christmas at Pops
The Joy of Christmas

CHRISTMAS EVE, 1975

Tony Orlando and Dawn
A Bicentennial Christmas
The Oral Roberts Christmas Special

CHRISTMAS EVE, 1976

Donny and Marie
The Homecoming: A Christmas Story
The Sounds of Christmas

CHRISTMAS, EVE, 1977

The Jeffersons
A Special Christmas with Mr. Rogers
Christmas Around the World

CHRISTMAS EVE, 1978
The Nutcracker
It Happened One Christmas
Amahl and the Night Visitors

CHRISTMAS EVE, 1979
A Christmas Special . . . With Love, Mac Davis
Christmas Eve on Sesame Street
Family

CHRISTMAS EVE, 1980
The House Without a Christmas Tree
A Fat Albert Christmas
Real People

CHRISTMAS EVE, 1981
High Hopes: The Capra Years
20/20
The Man in the Santa Claus Suit

CHRISTMAS EVE, 1982
Pinocchio's Christmas
The Nativity
The Muppet Movie

CHRISTMAS EVE, 1983
Diff'rent Strokes
Christmas with Luciano Pavarotti
The Love Boat

CHRISTMAS EVE, 1984
Sleeping Beauty
Cagney and Lacey
Scarecrow and Mrs. King

CHRISTMAS EVE, 1985
Sing-It-Yourself Messiah
The Black Stallion
Joyeux Noël: A Cajun Christmas

CHRISTMAS EVE, 1986
The Night They Saved Christmas
St. Elsewhere
Robert Shaw's Christmas Special

CHRISTMAS EVE, 1987
Bugs Bunny's Looney Christmas Tales
The Magic Flute
Oprah!

CHRISTMAS EVE, 1988

A Claymation Christmas Celebration

Christmas Comes to Willow Creek

The Garfield Christmas Special

CHRISTMAS EVE, 1989

A Christmas Carol

A Muppet Family Christmas

Bill Cosby Salutes Alvin Ailey

CHRISTMAS EVE, 1990

A Very Retail Christmas

The New Visions Christmas Special

A Child's Christmas in Wales

CHRISTMAS EVE, 1991

The Little Match Girl

The Tailor of Gloucester

Die Fledermaus

CHRISTMAS EVE, 1992

The Night Before Christmas

Christmas in Vienna

It's a Wonderful Life

CHRISTMAS EVE, 1993

Disney's Christmas Fantasy on Ice

Scrooge

The Christmas Star

CHRISTMAS EVE, 1994

National Football League Playoffs

Christmas Carol

Hallelujah

CHRISTMAS EVE, 1995

Cincinnati Pops Orchestra

Seasons Greetings from the Honeymooners

The Honeymooner's First Christmas

WHY DOES *Santa* WEAR RED?

WHY TWELVE DAYS? A SECRET MESSAGE IN THE SONG?

Some Christians attach certain symbolism to specific gifts mentioned in the verses of the song "The Twelve Days of Christmas." For example, for them the meaning of the partridge in the pear tree is God or Jesus. The two turtledoves equate with the two parts of the Bible—the Old Testament and the New Testament. The three French hens correlate to the Trinity of the Father, Son, and Holy Spirit. The four calling birds are the names of the four Gospels (Matthew, Mark, Luke, and John). The five gold rings represent the Pentateuch (first five books of the Old Testament). Six geese a-laying are the six days in which God made Creation. Seven swans are the seven sacraments or the seven gifts bestowed by the Holy Spirit. Eight maids equate with the eight Beatitudes of which Jesus spoke. Nine ladies are the nine fruits of the Holy Spirit. Ten lords a-leaping are the Ten Commandments that God gave to Moses. Eleven pipers piping represent the eleven Apostles, and the twelve drummers drumming are seen as the twelve doctrines found in the Apostle's Creed. No one can know for sure if the writer(s) of this song meant for these analogies—it's just a theory, what do you think?

Why Not Eleven?:
"The Twelve Days of Christmas"

"The Twelve Days of Christmas," traditional British song

On the **first day** of Christmas my true love sent to me
A partridge in a pear tree.

On the **second day** of Christmas my true love sent to me
Two turtledoves and a partridge in a pear tree.

On the **third day** of Christmas my true love sent to me
Three French hens, two turtledoves, and a partridge in a pear tree.

On the **fourth day** of Christmas my true love sent to me
Four calling birds, three French hens, two turtledoves, and a partridge in a pear tree.

On the **fifth day** of Christmas my true love sent to me
Five gold rings, four calling birds, three French hens, two turtledoves, and a partridge in a pear tree.

On the **sixth day** of Christmas my true love sent to me
Six geese a-laying, five gold rings, four calling birds . . .

On the **seventh day** of Christmas my true love sent to me
Seven swans a-swimming, six geese a laying . . .

On the **eighth day** of Christmas my true love sent to me
Eight maids a-milking . . .

On the **ninth day** of Christmas my true love sent to me
Nine ladies dancing . . .

On the **tenth day** of Christmas my true love sent to me
Ten lords a-leaping . . .

On the **eleventh day** of Christmas my true love sent to me
Eleven pipers piping . . .

On the **twelfth day** of Christmas my true love sent to me
Twelve drummers drumming . . .

In its earliest form, the carol was a Hebrew hymn designed to be sung as a dialgoue between a choir and their cantor. The medievals rewrote the song from Hebrew into Latin and utilized images of Christmas.

part eleven

sugar plums dancing:
recipes for the season

*F*ood is central to the celebration of the Christmas holiday—and no book on the subject of celebrating Christmas would really be complete without a sampling of holiday recipes. Here are a few favorites. Some are for Christmas morning, some are for the big meal of the big day, and some can be adapted to other times. Enjoy these great meals in the spirit of the holiday, with friends and family—Bon appetit!

OFF TO A GOOD START: BREAKFAST AND BRUNCH

Cranberry Bread

A WHOLESOME AND DELICIOUS HOLIDAY TREAT—AND EASY TO MAKE, TOO!

2 cups all-purpose flour
1 cup granulated sugar
1½ teaspoons baking powder
½ teaspoon baking soda
1 teaspoon salt
¼ cup shortening
½ cup orange juice
1 teaspoon grated orange peel
1 large egg, lightly beaten
1 cup frozen cranberries, chopped into halves
½ cup chopped walnuts

1. Preheat oven to 350 degrees Fahrenheit. Grease a 9″ × 5″ loaf pan.

2. Sift together flour, sugar, baking powder, baking soda, and salt.

3. Using a pastry blender or two knives held together, cut in shortening until coarse crumbs form.

4. In a separate bowl, combine orange juice, orange peel, and egg.

5. Make a well in the center of the dry ingredients. Add egg mixture all at once to well, tossing with a fork until just moistened.

6. Stir in the nuts and cranberries. Spread batter in prepared pan. Bake until a toothpick inserted in the center comes out clean, approximately 1 hour.

7. Remove bread from pan; cool completely.

Crisp Waffles for Christmas Morning

FOR A HOLIDAY ACCENT, TOP THESE WITH WHIPPED CREAM AND GREEN AND RED CRYSTAL SUGAR.

2 cups sifted cake flour
4 teaspoons baking powder
¼ teaspoon salt
2 large eggs
1¼ cup plus 1 tablespoon milk
6 tablespoons vegetable oil or melted butter

1. Grease and preheat an electric waffle iron.

2. Sift together the dry ingredients.

3. Beat the eggs with an electric mixer.

4. Add milk and dry ingredients alternately until just blended.

5. Stir in oil or melted butter.

6. Spoon batter onto prepared waffle iron and cook until golden brown and crisp. (Cooking times will vary.)

Eggs a la Buckingham

A GREAT—AND EASY—PREPARATION FOR CHRISTMAS MORNING.

5 large eggs, lightly beaten
½ cup milk
½ teaspoon salt
⅓ teaspoon pepper
5 slices toasted white bread
1 tablespoon butter
Grated cheddar cheese to taste

1. Arrange toast slices in a baking dish or ovenproof platter.

2. In a large bowl, combine eggs with milk, salt, and pepper.

3. Melt butter in skillet; cook eggs until just scrambled. (They should appear slightly undercooked.)

4. Spoon eggs over toast; sprinkle with grated cheddar cheese.

5. Bake until cheese melts, approximately five minutes.

6. Serve immediately.

Fancy Nancy's Christmas Irish Bundt Bread

AN UNFORGETTABLE HOLIDAY TREAT THE WHOLE FAMILY CAN ENJOY!

3 cups all-purpose flour
3 teaspoons baking powder
¾ cup granulated sugar
1½ cups milk
⅓ cup vegetable oil
1 egg
1 cup golden raisins, tightly packed
1 tablespoon caraway seeds

For icing:
1 cup confectioner's sugar, sifted
1½ tablespoons hot water or milk
½ teaspoon vanilla flavoring
Green or red food coloring

1. Preheat oven to 350 degrees Fahrenheit. Grease and flour a 9-inch Bundt pan.

2. In food processor, combine flour, baking powder, and sugar and process.

3. In a large bowl, mix together milk, oil, and egg.

4. Pour liquid mixture into food processor with flour mixture; pulse until blended and smooth.

5. Pour mixture back into mixing bowl. Add raisins and caraway seeds. Mix well.

6. Pour batter into prepared pan.

7. Bake bread until a toothpick inserted into the center comes out clean, 35 to 45 minutes. Cool for 25 minutes in pan. Cool for 1 hour on rack.

8. Mix icing ingredients together and drizzle over bread.

German Coffee Cake

A TRADITIONAL FAVORITE.

1 cup margarine, softened
2 cups granulated sugar
4 large eggs, at room temperature
1 pint sour cream
2 teaspoons vanilla extract
2 teaspoons baking soda
1½ cups all-purpose flour
3 teaspoons baking powder
½ cup walnuts

Topping:
½ cup granulated sugar and 2 teaspoons cinnamon,
   mixed together in small bowl

1. Preheat oven to 350 degrees Fahrenheit. Grease a 9″ × 13″ baking pan.

2. In a large mixing bowl, cream together margarine and sugar.

3. Add eggs, sour cream, baking soda, and vanilla.

4. Beat in flour and baking powder. Stir in nuts.

5. Pour half of the batter into a greased 9″ × 13″ pan.

6. Sprinkle half of the topping over batter; run a knife once through batter.

7. Pour remaining batter into pan, then run a knife once through batter.

8. Bake until a toothpick inserted into the center comes out clean, approximately 40 to 45 minutes.

9. Transfer baking pan onto a wire rack. Cool for 30 minutes.

BREAKFAST AND BRUNCH ENTERTAINING TIPS

Whether your family's tradition on Christmas morning is to sit down together to an opulent breakfast or go a little lighter in favor of a sumptuous brunch, there are some things you can do to make the meal run more smoothly and be less work for you. Here are a few tips: Do everything you can the night before (okay, the night before is Christmas Eve and you may be a little busy, so do it the afternoon before). Set a menu. Purchase the things you'll need to cook. Whenever you have time, set up your morning table using Christmas placemats and holiday-themed tableware, with napkins slipped into pretty holiday napkin rings. Add a festive centerpiece, utensils, juice glasses, and mugs for coffee and cocoa. Put a basket with a pretty towel in it on the table to hold breads and assorted sweet rolls. Make sure that salt-and-pepper shakers, the butter dish, and cream and sugar are on the table. Cover the table with another cloth to keep everything clean, and china dust-free, until you get up on Christmas morning.

For a brunch with family and friends, think buffet. Decide on a menu and make what you can ahead of time. Prepare your table on the day before the buffet. Make it festive using pretty Christmas linens, decorated candlesticks with candles, and a centerpiece. Either set the table with your china or stack plates in a convenient area near the food. Silverware can go near the plates in holiday baskets. Figure out a seating arrangement, attach place cards onto candy canes and put one at each plate setting. On the buffet or a side table, position things like serving bowls, platters, a compartmentalized food warmer and soufflé dishes, a punch bowl for alcoholic punch or a container to hold iced champagne, a pitcher for juice, and a large coffee pot.

(You can put the coffee in the filter the night before and then in the morning, just add water and turn it on.) On a pretty tray, place a cream pitcher, sugar bowl, and an assortment of teas. Special dishes like a cranberry frozen soufflé with a mint and berry wreath can be made a day ahead and removed just before the buffet meal begins.

~~◦~~

FOR PARTIES AND FAMILY DINNERS, APPETIZERS AND SIDES SURE TO PLEASE

Antipasto

AN EXQUISITE DELIGHT!

1 pound American cheese, sliced

½ pound imported ham, sliced

1 two-pound imported Genoa salami, sliced

½ pound prosciutto, sliced

½ pound mortadella, sliced

1 12 oz. can tuna, packed in oil (not drained)

1 full head lettuce

½ pound imported sharp provolone, cut into 1-inch chunks

1 8 oz. jar pepperoncini

1 8 oz. can green stuffed olives

Olive oil

Red wine vinegar

1. Roll slices of meat with American cheese and line along the outside of a large platter, alternating the different kinds of meat.

2. Wash, dry, and break up the lettuce and arrange in the center of the plate.

3. Spread tuna on top of lettuce, being sure not to drain any oil from the can.

4. Arrange provolone around the lettuce.

5. Top with olives and peppers.

Dressing

Mix together three parts olive oil to one part red wine vinegar. Pass separately to guests.

Crispy Christmas Nachos

ONDELE!

½ cup yellow cornmeal
½ teaspoon salt
1¾ cups boiling water
1 teaspoon margarine

1. Preheat oven to 425 degrees Fahrenheit. Grease a baking sheet.

2. Mix cornmeal and salt in a bowl. Mix in 1 cup of boiling water. Blend.

3. Add margarine, stirring until melted; add remaining water; stir.

4. Drop mixture by rounded teaspoonful (drop should be a little bigger than a quarter) onto prepared baking sheet.

5. Bake nachos until golden and crisp, 12 to 15 minutes or until golden brown. Serve with salsa.

Holiday Shrimp Dip

DELICIOUS AND ELEGANT!

3 cans small deveined shrimp, drained
2 8 oz. packages cream cheese, softened
1 12 oz. bottle shrimp sauce
Crackers of your choice
Parsley

1. Combine shrimp and cream cheese.

2. Add ½ bottle shrimp sauce and mix well. Place shrimp mixture in mold of appropriate size.

3. Chill overnight.

4. Invert mold onto a platter. Spoon remaining sauce over top as if frosting.

5. Garnish with parsley and serve with crackers.

WHY DOES *Santa* WEAR RED?

California Yorkshire Pudding

A NEW TWIST ON AN OLD FAVORITE.

¼ cup pan drippings reserved from roast beef
6 large eggs
2 cups milk
1½ teaspoons salt
1½ teaspoons Worcestershire sauce
1½ cups all-purpose flour
2½ cups cooked and cooled wild rice

1. Preheat oven to 450 degrees Fahrenheit.

2. Pour one teaspoon of the pan drippings into twelve muffin-pan cups. Place muffin pan in prepared oven for two and a half minutes.

3. Mix together eggs, milk, salt, and Worcestershire sauce in a large bowl; blend until mixed well. Add flour, stirring until blended.

4. Add rice. Pour batter evenly into the hot drippings in prepared pan. Bake until brown and puffy, approximately 25 minutes.

Creamy Sweet Potato Soufflé

YOU'LL NEVER THINK OF THE HUMBLE SWEET POTATO IN QUITE THE SAME WAY
AFTER SAMPLING THIS HOLIDAY TREAT.

¼ cup butter
½ cup all-purpose flour
1½ cups half-and-half
5 large eggs (room temperature), separated
½ cup grated Cheddar cheese
1½ teaspoons salt
3 cloves garlic, crushed
½ teaspoon pepper
¼ teaspoon cream of tartar
1½ cups cold mashed sweet potatoes

1. Preheat oven to 375 degrees Fahrenheit.

2. Grease a 2-quart soufflé dish with a collar extending 3 inches above
the rim.

3. Melt butter in a large saucepan. Mix in flour and cook. Stirring constantly, for 1 minute. Blend in the half-and-half; cook over low heat, stirring constantly.

4. Stir in egg yolks, 1 at a time. Stir in cheese, salt, garlic, and pepper,
beating well after each addition.

5. Stir mashed potatoes into the egg mixture.

6. In a large bowl, beat the egg whites with cream of tartar until stiff peaks form. Fold egg whites into potato mixture.

7. Pour potato mixture into prepared dish.

8. Bake soufflé until top is puffy and golden, approximately 50 minutes. Serve immediately.

HOSTING A CROWD If you are hosting a party for a large group, advance planning is a must. Not only will the food and drink be important, but so will seating and activities. Some questions to ask yourself might include these: How many people are coming? What will be the activities? Will the furniture need to be rearranged to accommodate the guests? Are there enough chairs? Is the parking sufficient? What about doing a toy drive? How far in advance of the party does the food need to be prepared? Which traditional dishes are easy to prepare and liked by most everyone? Turkey and ham come to mind, oh, and meatballs, too. In the next section, you'll find recipes for all three as well as a couple of excellent stuffings to try.

CELEBRATORY MAIN COURSES AND ACCOMPANIMENTS

Breadcrumb Stuffing

A POPULAR STUFFING RECIPE.

1⅓ tablespoon butter, melted
3 cups seasoned breadcrumbs
¾ teaspoon salt
½ teaspoon pepper
1⅓ tablespoons dried parsley
8 drops onion juice
1 large egg, beaten well

1.   In a large mixing bowl, drizzle butter over breadcrumbs. Toss together with a fork.

2.   Stir in salt, pepper, dried parsley, and onion juice. Mix well.

3.   Mix in beaten egg.

4.   Stuff poultry just prior to cooking. (You may wish to increase the quantities in the recipe if you are cooking a particularly large bird.)

Christmas Sweet and Sour Meatballs

A MEMORABLE HOLIDAY ENTRÉE.

1 pound ground beef, chicken, or turkey
1 cup seasoned breadcrumbs
1 large egg, lightly beaten
2 tablespoons chopped onion
2 tablespoons milk
¾ teaspoon salt
2 tablespoons solid vegetable shortening
1 8¼ ounce can pineapple chunks, drained (reserve the juice!)
1 tablespoon cornstarch
¼ cup cold water
1 8 ounce can whole or jellied cranberry sauce
Half of a 12 oz. bottle barbecue sauce
¼ teaspoon salt
½ medium green bell pepper, cut in strips

1. Mix ground meat, breadcrumbs, egg, onion, milk, and salt in a large mixing bowl. Using a tablespoon, shape meat mixture into meatballs.

2. In a medium bowl, mix together shortening, pineapple chunks, cranberry sauce, barbecue sauce, and salt.

3. In a second bowl, dissolve cornstarch in cold water.

4. In a large skillet, cook meatballs until browned. Drain off grease.

5. Stir pineapple and cornstarch mixture into the skillet.

6. Add pepper strips. Simmer, covered, until peppers are tender, 15 to 20 minutes, making sure peppers become tender. Add reserved pineapple juice a little at a time, until mixture reaches desired consistency.

Glazed Yule Ham

NOT TO BE MISSED.

10- to 15-pound uncooked store-bought ham
Orange marmalade
1 8-ounce package of cream cheese, softened
Greens of your choice (for garnish)

1. Follow package directions for baking ham. (Generally, baking takes 3½ to 4 hours.)

2. 30 minutes before ham is done, brush over with orange marmalade.

3. Transfer ham to a cutting board. Cool slightly.

4. Using a pastry bag fitted with a star tip, pipe cream cheese decoratively on top of ham.

5. Slice and garnish with greens.

WHY DOES *Santa* WEAR RED?

Holiday Maple Ham

THE REAL THING.

1¼ cups firmly packed dark brown sugar
⅓ cup maple syrup
Whole cloves (quantity will depend on size of ham)
Precooked ham (approximately ten pounds), trimmed

1. Preheat oven to 350 degrees Farenheit.

2. In a medium bowl, combine the brown sugar and the maple syrup.

3. Place the ham on a rack in a roasting pan, and place the pan in the center rack of the oven. Bake for an hour and ten minutes.

4. Transfer the ham from the oven to the counter; using a kitchen knife, score the surface of the ham in a diamond pattern.

5. Insert cloves evenly along top of the ham.

6. Brush brown sugar and maple syrup mixture over ham.

7. Return ham to oven; bake for 20 minutes more.

Sausage, Poultry, and Game Stuffing

ANOTHER DISTINCTIVE STUFFING RECIPE.

¾ cup sausage, uncooked, casings removed, crumbled
2½ cups seasoned breadcrumbs
4 cups water
1¼ tablespoons dried parsley
1½ tablespoons dried onion
½ teaspoon pepper
2 large eggs, lightly beaten
⅓ cup butter, melted

1. In a skillet, brown sausage lightly. Remove sausage; drain on a paper towel.

2. Place breadcrumbs in a large bowl and add four cups of water.

3. When the breadcrumbs are soft, press out excess liquid by hand.

4. In a large bowl, combine sausage with soft breadcrumbs, parsley, onion, pepper, and beaten eggs.

5. Drizzle melted butter into sausage mixture.

6. Stuff poultry just prior to cooking. (You may wish to increase the quantities in the recipe if you are cooking a particularly large bird.)

A FLAWLESS CHRISTMAS FEAST Leaving dessert off a Christmas feast is like forgetting to embellish the tree with ornaments. Every flawless feast needs a great finish! For the non-chocolate lovers and the chocolate-lovers alike, the next section offers some tasty cookie recipes and one for gingerbread. Um-um-m, go ahead, indulge. Christmas comes but once a year. Here's an easy little bourbon pecan ball to get you started.

SWEETS EVEN SCROOGE WOULD LOVE

Chocolate Bourbon Balls with Pecans

A SOUTHERN CHRISTMAS FAVORITE.

¾ cup powdered sugar, plus 1 tablespoon
2 tablespoons unsweetened cocoa powder
2 cups vanilla wafers, crushed
½ cup toasted pecans, finely chopped
⅓ cup bourbon
3 tablespoons honey

1. Sift 1 tablespoon powdered sugar with cocoa in a small bowl.

2. Whisk to combine.

3. Combine crushed vanilla wafers with pecans.

4. Mix together bourbon, ¾ cup powdered sugar, and honey in a small bowl.

5. Pour bourbon mixture into the vanilla wafers mixture.

6. Stir to combine all ingredients.

7. Remove 1 teaspoon of the mixture at a time and form into a ball.

8. Roll balls in the cocoa mixture until all dough is used.

9. Layer balls in an airtight container, separating with sheets of wax paper.

10. Store in a cool, dry place for one week before serving.

Chocolate Caramels

A HOLIDAY DELIGHT FOR CHOCOLATE LOVERS.

2½ tablespoons butter
2 cups molasses
1 cup firmly packed dark brown sugar
½ cup milk
3 ounces semisweet chocolate, coarsely chopped
1 teaspoon vanilla extract

1. In medium-sized saucepan, melt butter over medium heat.

2. Add molasses, brown sugar, vanilla, and milk. Stir until sugar is dissolved.

3. Bring mixture to a simmer; add chocolate, stirring until melted and smooth.

4. Bring chocolate mixture to a boil. Remove from heat for a moment and test. When a small amount of the mixture is dropped in cold water, and a firm ball can be formed, proceed to next step. Do not overcook!

5. Pour mixture into medium-sized buttered pan.

6. Let stand until cool; cut into small squares.

Christmas Cutout Cookies

HEAVEN IN ICING.

½ cup butter
½ cup granulated sugar
2 large eggs, lightly beaten
1 teaspoon vanilla extract
¼ cup sliced almonds
2 teaspoons baking powder
2¾ cups all-purpose flour
Green and red colored sugar
Icing (commercially prepared, in tubes)

1. Preheat oven to 400 degrees Fahrenheit.

2. In a mixing bowl, beat together butter and sugar until light and fluffy.

3. Beat in eggs, vanilla, and almonds.

4. Beat in baking powder and flour, ½ cup at a time until blended.

5. Wrap dough in plastic wrap and chill for several hours.

6. On a floured surface, using a floured rolling pin, roll out dough.

7. Using several different shaped cookie cutters, cut out cookies.

8. Bake cookies until just golden, approximately 6–7 minutes.

9. Decorate with colored sugar and icing.

Coconut Wreath Cookies

A REAL SIGN THAT THE CHRISTMAS SEASON IS IN FULL SWING!

½ cup butter or margarine, softened
½ cup granulated sugar
1 large egg
1 3½ ounce pack of shredded sweetened coconut
1¾ cups all-purpose flour
Red and green candied cherries, sliced

WHY DOES *Santa* WEAR RED?

1. Preheat oven to 375 degrees Fahrenheit.

2. Grease and flour a baking sheet.

3. In a large bowl, beat together butter and sugar.

4. Blend in egg and coconut. On low speed, add flour, ½ cup at a time, until blended.

5. Wrap dough in plastic wrap and chill for several hours.

6. On floured surface, roll ⅓ of dough at a time to a quarter-inch thickness. Using a 2 ½-inch doughnut cutter, cut dough into rings. Gather trimmings; roll out dough; cut more cookies.

7. Remove any excess coconut from edges; edges of cookies should be smooth.

8. Lightly grease and flour large cookie sheet. Place cookies on prepared baking sheet 1 inch apart.

9. Arrange cherry slices on cookies to resemble flower petals; press into cookies.

10. Bake cookies in batches for 10 minutes or until brown.

Gingerbread from Home

REAL HOME-STYLE GINGERBREAD—PERFECT FOR HOLIDAY SNACKS!

½ cup firmly packed light brown sugar
⅓ cup butter
1 teaspoon baking soda
½ cup light molasses
1¼ cup all-purpose flour
1 teaspoon ground cinnamon
½ teaspoon ground ginger
1 large egg, beaten
½ cup boiling water

1. Preheat oven to 325 degrees Fahrenheit.

2. Grease and flour an 8-inch square baking pan.

3. In a bowl, mix together brown sugar, butter, baking soda, and molasses.

4. Add flour, cinnamon, and ginger. Mix well.

5. Add in egg and boiling water. Mix well.

6. Pour batter into prepared pan; smooth top.

7. Bake gingerbread until a toothpick inserted into the center comes out clean, approximately 40 minutes.

WHY DOES *Santa* WEAR RED?

WHAT TO DO WITH ALL THOSE COOKIES! You can use the leftover cookies to make a trifle, that stunningly beautiful English dessert that features layers of custard, macaroons drenched in brandy or other liqueurs, a layer of fruit, a puree or jam, mascarpone or whipping cream, layers of sponge cake, and sometimes slivered almonds or glazed cherries and served in a clear glass pedestal dish (so you can admire all those layers).

A simple version of trifle uses pound cake, lemon curd, whipping cream, fresh large sliced strawberries, and strawberry sauce but no liqueur. The steps are simple: Slice the cake horizontally in half and place one half in a trifle bowl. Add half the sauce, add half the berries, pour half the lemon curd over the berries, cover with half the whipped cream. Repeat the steps. Cover and refrigerate overnight. Sprinkle with slivered almonds before serving. Any combinations of sweets should taste yummy in this dessert. You can mix and match ingredients, depending on the cookies you have left over, to make your very own recipe for trifle. Enjoy!

Or, you could work your way through a tin of leftover cookies by simply dipping them into some drinks to chase the winter chill away. For some yummy drinks to warm your soul, keep on reading!

DRINKS TO WARM THE SOUL

Brandy Cocoa

A MELLOW AND DELICIOUS DRINK FOR THE HOLIDAYS.

4 cups whole milk
2 tablespoons unsweetened cocoa powder
⅓ cup granulated sugar
1½ cups boiling water
3 teaspoons brandy

1. In a saucepan, scald milk.

2. In another saucepan, mix cocoa, sugar, and enough boiling water to make a smooth paste.

3. Add remaining water and boil one minute, then add to milk.

4. Mix well; add brandy, then beat mixture for two minutes.

5. Serve in large mugs.

WHY DOES *Santa* WEAR RED?

Cranberry Glogg

A NEW ENGLAND FAVORITE. IT'S FUNNY TO SAY AND GREAT TO DRINK. THIS IS A WARMHEARTED CUP OF HOLIDAY CHEER GUARANTEED TO START EVEN THE COLDEST EVENING OFF RIGHT.

6 cups cranberry juice cocktail
6 whole cloves
2 cinnamon sticks
Cinnamon schnapps to taste

1. Combine juice, cloves, and cinnamon in a large saucepan.

2. Warm over medium heat for 15 minutes. Reduce heat and let sit for 5 minutes.

3. Remove cinnamon sticks and cloves.

4. Pour into mugs.

5. Add schnapps as desired, depending on the amount of warmth you have in mind.

Homemade Coffee Liqueur for Christmas,

Begun in November

THE TROPICAL STUFF YOU BUY IN THE STORE IS PRETTY GOOD, BUT OUR GUESS IS YOU'LL GET MORE OF A KICK OUT OF PUTTING THIS VARIATION TOGETHER YOURSELF. TRY IT. IT TAKES SOME TIME, BUT IT'S WORTH IT. YOU MAY NEVER GO BACK TO THE LABELED VERSION AGAIN.

4 cups granulated sugar
2 ounces instant coffee crystals
2 cups water
3 cups vodka
1 vanilla bean, split in half lengthwise

1. Mix sugar and coffee in the bottom of a large pitcher.

2. Add water.

3. Chill for 90 minutes, then add vodka. Mix well.

4. Drop the vanilla bean into an empty half-gallon bottle with a screw top.

5. Pour the coffee mixture into the bottle, seal, and store for 30 days in a dark place.

WHY DOES *Santa* WEAR RED?

Hot Candy Cane in a Holiday Mug

COCOA MADE FROM SCRATCH IS BEST, BUT PREPARED MIXES TO WHICH YOU ADD
BOILING WATER WILL SERVE, TOO.

Two cups hot cocoa
Peppermint liqueur
Whipped cream
Two red maraschino cherries, halved
Two green maraschino cherries, halved

1. Pour hot cocoa into 2 large mugs.

3. Add peppermint liqueur to taste.

4. Top with whipped cream and red and green maraschino cherries.

Perfect Eggnog

EASY TO MAKE AND MUCH BETTER THAN
THE STORE-BOUGHT STUFF.

6 large eggs, separated
½ cup granulated sugar
1 pint heavy cream
1 pint milk
1 pint whiskey
2 ounces rum

1. Place egg yolks in a large bowl.

2. Add sugar to the yolks, beating at medium speed.

3. After the yolks have been beaten very stiff, mix the egg whites with the yolk mixture.

4. Stir in cream and milk.

5. Add whiskey and rum. Stir thoroughly.

6. Chill for 2 hours. Serve with grated nutmeg on top.

Why So Silent?:
"Silent Night"

"SILENT NIGHT," BY JOSEPH MOHR (1792–1848)

Silent night, holy night!
All is calm, all is bright
Round yon Virgin Mother and Child
Holy Infant, so tender and mild,
Sleep in heavenly peace,
Sleep in heavenly peace.

Silent night, holy night!
Shepherds quake at the sight,
Glories stream from heaven afar,
Heav'nly hosts sing alleluia!
Christ the Saviour is born!
Christ the Saviour is born!

Silent night, holy night!
Wondrous star, lend thy light!
With the angels, let us sing
Alleluia to our King!
Christ the Saviour is here,
Jesus the Saviour is here.

"Stille Nacht! Heilige Nacht" (popularly known as "Silent Night"), is one of the best-loved Christmas carols of all time. It has been translated into many languages and dialects of countries around the world. The first time it was sung, however, was in 1818 in a tiny village in Oberndorf, Bavaria. The parishioners were gathered for midnight Mass in St. Nicholas Church. A young priest named Josef Mohr had composed the poem two years earlier and had asked his friend Franz Xaver Gruber, the choir director, to write a tune that Mohr could perform with his guitar.

Tradition has it that since the guitar was associated with drinking music, Gruber didn't want to do it; however, the church organ was broken (or so the story goes). So Gruber wrote an arrangement for the guitar and then Mohr performed the music with the help of the choir on Christmas Eve in 1818. There were six verses in all, and the choir, in four-part harmony repeated the last two lines of each of the verses.

Mohr and Gruber did various arrangements of the song between 1820 and 1855. A family of singers known as The Strassers performed the song in 1832 at a concert in Leipzig. The song became the favorite of heads of state and common people alike throughout Europe and the world. Mohr died in 1848 and was buried in the tiny community of Wagrain. His friend Gruber died years later and was buried in Hallein. His gravesite features a decorated tree each Christmas season. By 1955, "Silent Night," according to some sources, had become such a world favorite that it achieved the status of the most-recorded song of all time.

part twelve

a literary look
at christmas

*T*he following sample of classic Christmas storytelling runs from Dickens to Twain, touching new and old works in between. These read-aloud holiday tales will enchant you and your family during the holiday season. Why not read a little to each other while sitting in front of the fire sipping hot cocoa? You and your family will be sure to enjoy these festive favorites!

The Little Women's Christmas

by Louisa May Alcott

PUBLISHED IN 1868, *LITTLE WOMEN* WAS AN INSTANT SUCCESS, PARTICULARLY WITH FEMALE READERS OF THE TIME. HERE IS AN EXCERPT FROM THE FIRST FEW CHAPTERS OF THE BOOK. THE LITTLE WOMEN THEMSELVES STAND AS A REMINDER TO ALL WHO HAVE ENDURED HARD TIMES THAT EVEN A PENNILESS CHRISTMAS CAN BE CAUSE FOR CELEBRATION . . . IF IT IS FILLED WITH SELFLESS GENEROSITY, LOVE, AND FAITH.

Jo was the first to wake in the gray dawn of Christmas morning. No stockings hung at the fireplace, and for a moment she felt as much disappointed as she did long ago, when her little sock fell down because it was so crammed with goodies. Then she remembered her mother's promise, and slipping her hand under her pillow, drew out a little crimson-covered book. She knew it very well, for it was that beautiful old story of the best life ever lived, and Jo felt that it was a true guidebook for any pilgrim going the long journey. She woke Meg with a "Merry Christmas," and bade her see what was under her pillow. A green-covered book appeared, with the same picture inside, and a few words written by their mother, which made their one present very precious in their eyes. Presently Beth and Amy woke, to rummage and find their little books also—one dove-colored, the other blue; and all sat looking at and talking about them, while the East grew rosy with the coming day.

"Girls," said Meg, seriously, looking from the tumbled head beside her to the two little night-capped ones in the room beyond, "Mother wants us to read and love and mind these books, and we must begin at once. We used to be faithful about it; but since Father went away, and all this war trouble unsettled us, we have neglected many things. You can do as you please; but I shall keep my book on the table here, and read a little every morning as soon as I wake, for I know it will do me good, and help me through the day."

Then she opened her new book and began to read. Jo put her arm around her, and, leaning cheek to cheek, read also, with the quiet expression so seldom seen on her restless face.

"How good Meg is! Come, Amy, let's do as they do. I'll help you with the hard words, and they'll explain things if we don't understand," whispered Beth, very impressed by the pretty books and her sister's example.

"I'm glad mine is blue," said Amy; and then the rooms were very still while the pages were softly turned, and the winter sunshine crept in to touch the bright heads and serious faces with a Christmas greeting.

"Where is Mother?" asked Meg as she and Jo ran down to thank her for their gifts, half an hour later.

"Goodness only knows. Some poor creeter come a-beggin', and your ma went straight off to see what was needed. There never was such a woman for givin' away vittles and drink, clothes, and firin'," replied Hannah, who had lived with the family since Meg was born, and was considered by them all more as a friend than a servant.

"She will be back soon, I guess; so do your cakes, and have everything ready," said Meg, looking over the presents which were collected in a basket and kept under the sofa, ready to be produced at the proper time. "Why, where is Amy's bottle of cologne?" she added, as the little flask did not appear.

"She took it out a minute ago, and went off with it to put a ribbon on it, or some such notion," replied Jo, dancing about the room to take the first stiffness off the new army-slippers.

"How nice my handkerchiefs look, don't they? Hannah washed and ironed them for me, and I marked them all myself," said Beth, looking proudly at the somewhat uneven letters which had cost her such labor.

"Bless the child, she's gone and put 'Mother' on them instead of 'M. March'; how funny!" cried Jo, taking up one.

"Isn't it right? I thought it was better to do it so because Meg's initials are 'M. M.' and I don't want any one to use these but Marmee," said Beth, looking troubled.

"It's all right, dear, and a very pretty idea; quite sensible, too, for no one can ever mistake them now. It will please her very much, I know," said Meg, with a frown for Jo, and a smile for Beth.

"There's Mother; hide the basket, quick!" cried Jo, as a door slammed, and steps sounded in the hall.

Amy came in hastily, and looked rather abashed when she saw her sisters all waiting for her.

"Where have you been, and what are you hiding behind you?" asked Meg, surprised to see, by her hood and cloak, that lazy Amy had been out so early.

"Don't laugh at me, Jo. I didn't mean any one should know till the time came. I only meant to change the little bottle for a big one, and I gave all my money to get it, and I'm truly trying not to be selfish any more."

As she spoke, Amy showed the handsome flask which replaced the cheap one; and looked so earnest and humble in her little effort to forget herself, that Meg hugged her on the spot, and Jo pronounced her "a trump," while Beth ran to the window, and picked her finest rose to ornament the stately bottle.

"You see, I felt ashamed of my present, after reading and talking about being good this morning, so I ran round the corner and changed it the minute I was up; and I'm glad, for mine is the handsomest now."

Another bang of the street-door sent the basket under the sofa, and the girls to the table eager for breakfast.

"Merry Christmas, Marmee! Lots of them! Thank you for our books; we read some, and mean to every day," they cried in chorus.

"Merry Christmas, little daughters! I'm glad you began at once, and hope you will keep on. But I want to say one word before we sit down. Not far away from here lies a poor woman with a little new-born baby. Six children are huddled into one bed to keep from freezing, for they have no fire. There is nothing to eat over there; and the oldest boy came to tell me they were suffering hunger and cold. My girls, will you give them your breakfast as a Christmas present?"

They were all unusually hungry, having waited nearly an hour, and for a minute no one spoke; only a minute, for Jo exclaimed impetuously, "I'm so glad you came before we began!"

"May I go and help carry the things to the poor little children?" asked Beth, eagerly.

"I shall take the cream and the muffins," added Amy, heroically giving up the articles she most liked.

Meg was already covering the buckwheats, and piling the bread into one big plate.

"I thought you'd do it," said Mrs. March, smiling as if satisfied. "You shall all go and help me, and when we come back we will have bread and milk for breakfast, and make it up at dinner-time."

They were soon ready, and the procession set out. Fortunately it was early, and they went through back streets, so few people saw them, and no one laughed at the funny party.

A poor, bare, miserable room it was, with broken windows, no fire, ragged bedclothes, a sick mother, wailing baby, and a group of pale, hungry children cuddled under one old quilt, trying to keep warm. How the big eyes stared, and the blue lips smiled, as the girls went in!

"Ach, mein Gott! It is good angels come to us!" cried the poor woman, crying for joy.

"Funny angels in hoods and mittens," said Jo, and set them laughing.

In a few minutes it really did seem as if kind spirits had been at work there. Hannah, who had carried wood, made a fire, and stopped up the broken panes with old hats, and her own shawl. Mrs. March gave the mother tea and gruel, and comforted her with promises of help, while she dressed the little baby as tenderly as if it had been her own. The girls, meantime, spread the table, set the children round the fire, and fed them like so many hungry birds; laughing, talking, and trying to understand the funny broken English.

"Das ist gut!" "Die angel-kinder!" cried the poor things, as they ate, and warmed their purple hands at the comfortable blaze. The girls had never been called angel children before, and thought it very agreeable. That was a very happy breakfast, though they didn't get any of it; and when they went away, leaving comfort behind, I think there was not in all the city four merrier people than the hungry little girls who gave away their breakfasts, and contented themselves with bread and milk on Christmas morning.

"That's loving our neighbor better than ourselves, and I like it," said Meg, as they set out their presents, while their mother was upstairs collecting clothes for the poor Hummels.

Not a very splendid show, but there was a great deal of love done up in the few little bundles; and the tall vase of red roses, white chrysanthemums, and trailing vines, which stood in the middle, gave quite an elegant air to the table.

"She's coming! Strike up, Beth. Open the door, Amy. Three cheers for Marmee!" cried Jo, prancing about, while Meg went to conduct Mother to the seat of honor.

Beth played her gayest march, Amy threw open the door, and Meg enacted escort with great dignity. Mrs. March was both surprised and touched; and smiled with her eyes full as she examined her presents, and read the little notes which accompanied them. The slipper went on at once, a new handkerchief was slipped into her pocket, well scented with Amy's cologne, the rose was fastened in her bosom, and the nice gloves were pro-nounced "a perfect fit."

There was a good deal of laughing, and kissing, and explaining, in the simple, loving fashion which makes these home festivals so pleasant at the time and so sweet to remember long afterward.

Beth nestled up to her mother, and whispered softly, "I'm afraid Father isn't having such a merry Christmas as we are."

"Yes, Virginia, There Is a Santa Claus"

BY FRANCIS P. CHURCH FROM THE NEW YORK SUN, SEPTEMBER 21, 1897

EDITOR FRANCIS P. CHURCH'S LETTER TO VIRGINIA O'HANLON IS ONE OF THE MOST TOUCHING WRITTEN DEMONSTRATIONS OF THE IMPORTANCE IN BELIEVING IN WHAT CANNOT BE SEEN, TOUCHED, OR PROVEN. THE LETTER ORIGINALLY APPEARED IN THE SEPTEMBER 21, 1897, EDITION OF THE *NEW YORK SUN*. MORE THAN A CENTURY LATER, IT REMAINS A CLASSIC.

We take pleasure in answering at once and thus prominently the communication below, expressing at the same time our great gratification that its faithful author is numbered among the friends of the Sun:

> Dear Editor—I am 8 years old.
>
> Some of my little friends say there is no Santa Claus. Papa says 'If you see it in the Sun it's so.' Please tell me the truth, is there a Santa Claus?
>
> —Virginia O'Hanlon, 115 West Ninety-fifth street.

WHY DOES *Santa* WEAR RED?

Virginia, your little friends are wrong. They have been affected by the skepticism of a skeptical age. They do not believe except they see. They think that nothing can be which is not comprehensible by their little minds. All minds, Virginia, whether they be men's or children's are little. In this great universe of ours man is a mere insect, an ant, in his intellect, as compared with the boundless world about him, as measured by the intelligence capable of grasping the whole of truth and knowledge.

Yes, Virginia, there is a Santa Claus. He exists as certainly as love and generosity and devotion exist, and you know that they abound and give to your life its highest beauty and joy. Alas! How dreary would be the world if there were no Santa Claus! It would be as dreary as if there were no Virginias. There would be no childlike faith then, no poetry, no romance to make tolerable this existence. We should have no enjoyment, except in sense and sight. The eternal light with which childhood fills the world would be extinguished.

Not believe in Santa Claus! You might as well not believe in fairies! You might get your papa to hire men to watch in all the chimneys on Christmas Eve to catch Santa Claus, but even if they did not see Santa Claus coming down, what would that prove? Nobody sees Santa Claus, but that is no sign that there is no Santa Claus. The most real things in the world are those that neither children nor men can see. Did you ever see fairies dancing on the lawn? Of course not, but that's no proof that they are not there.

Nobody can conceive or imagine all the wonders there are unseen and unseeable in the world.

You tear apart the baby's rattle and see what makes the noise inside, but there is a veil covering the unseen world which not the strongest man, nor even the united strength of all the strongest men that ever lived, could tear apart. Only faith, fancy, poetry, love, romance, can push aside that curtain and view and picture the supernal beauty and glory beyond. Is it all real? Ah, Virginia, in all this world there is nothing else real and abiding.

No Santa Claus! Thank God! He lives, and he lives forever. A thousand years from now, Virginia, nay, ten times ten thousand years from now, he will continue to make glad the heart of childhood.

Excerpted from

A Christmas Carol

BY CHARLES DICKENS

WITH THE PUBLICATION IN 1843 OF *A CHRISTMAS CAROL IN PROSE* (AS THE FULL TITLE ORIGINALLY READ), CHARLES DICKENS BESTOWED A TIMELESS MESSAGE OF REPENTANCE AND HOPE TO GENERATIONS OF READERS. LORD JEFFREY, A DICKENS ENTHUSIAST, TOLD THE AUTHOR THAT HE HAD DONE "MORE GOOD BY THIS PUBLICATION, FOSTERED MORE KINDLY FEELINGS, AND PROMPTED MORE POSITIVE ACTS OF BENEFICENCE THAN CAN BE TRACED TO ALL THE PULPITS IN CHRISTENDOM SINCE CHRISTMAS 1842." THE 6,000-COPY FIRST PRINTING SOLD OUT IN A SINGLE DAY. OVER THE YEARS, DICKENS'S CLASSIC HAS BEEN ADAPTED INTO COUNTLESS MEDIA. WHAT FOLLOWS IS AN EXCERPT FROM THE FINAL PAGES OF THIS TRULY IMMORTAL WORK. THIS STORY LENDS ITSELF TO BEING READ ALOUD AMONG FRIENDS AND FAMILY, SO YOU CAN ALL ENJOY IT TOGETHER.

Yes! And the bedpost was his own. The bed was his own, the room was his own. Best and happiest of all, the Time before him was his own, to make amends in!

"I will live in the Past, the Present, and the Future!" Scrooge repeated, as he scrambled out of bed. "The Spirits of all three shall strive within me. Oh, Jacob Marley! Heaven, and the Christmas time be praised for this! I say it on my knees, old Jacob, on my knees!"

He was so fluttered and so glowing with his good intentions, that his broken voice would scarcely answer to his call. He had been sobbing violently in his conflict with the Spirit, and his face was wet with tears.

"They are not torn down," cried Scrooge, folding one of his bed curtains in his arms; "they are not torn down, rings and all. They are here—I am here—the shadows of the things that would have been may be dispelled. They will be. I know they will!"

His hands were busy with his garments all this time, turning them inside out, putting them on upside down, tearing them, mislaying them, making them parties to every kind of extravagance.

"I don't know what say of the month it is," said Scrooge. "I don't know how long I have been among the Spirits. I don't know anything. I'm quite a baby. Never mind. I don't care. I'd rather be a baby. Hallo! Whoop! Hallo here!"

He was checked in his transports by the churches ringing out the lustiest peals he had ever heard. Clash, clang, hammer; ding, dong, bell. Bell, dong, ding; hammer, clang, clash! Oh, glorious, glorious!

Running to the window, he opened it and put out his head. No fog, no mist; clear, bright, jovial, stirring, cold; cold, piping for the blood to dance to; golden sunlight; heavenly sky; sweet fresh air; merry bells. Oh, glorious. Glorious!

"What's today?" cried Scrooge, calling downward to a boy in Sunday clothes, who perhaps had loitered in to look about him.

"Eh?" returned the boy, with all his might of wonder.

"What's today, my fine fellow?" said Scrooge.

"Today!" replied the boy. "Why, Christmas Day."

"It's Christmas Day!" said Scrooge to himself. "I haven't missed it. The Spirits have done it all in one night. They can do anything they like. Of course they can. Of course they can. Hallo, my fine fellow!"

"Hallo!" returned the boy.

"Do you know the poulterer's in the next street but one, at the corner?" Scrooge inquired.

"I should hope I did," replied the lad.

"An intelligent boy!" said Scrooge. "A remarkable boy! Do you know whether they've sold the prize turkey that was hanging up there? Not the little prize turkey, the big one?"

"What, the one as big as me?" returned the boy.

"What a delightful boy!" said Scrooge. "It's a pleasure to talk to him. Yes, my buck!"

"It's hanging there now," replied the boy.

"Is it?" said Scrooge. "Go and buy it, and tell 'em to bring it here, that I may give them the direction where to take it. Come back with the man, and I'll give you a shilling. Come back with him in less than five minutes, and I'll you half a crown!"

The boy was off like a shot. He must have had a steady hand at a trigger who could have got a shot off half so fast.

"I'll send it to Bob Cratchit's," whispered Scrooge, rubbing his hands and splitting with a laugh. "He shan't know who sends it. It's twice the size of Tiny Tim. Joe Miller never made such a joke as sending it to Bob's will be!"

The hand in which he wrote the address was not a steady one, but write it he did, somehow, and went downstairs to open the street door, ready for the coming of the poulterer's man. As he stood there, waiting his arrival the knocker caught his eye.

"I shall love it as long as I live!" cried Scrooge, patting it with his hand. "I scarcely ever looked at it before. What an honest expression it has in its face! It's a wonderful knocker! Here's the turkey. Hallo! Whoop! How are you! Merry Christmas!"

It was a turkey. He never could have stood upon his legs, that bird. He would have snapped 'em short off in a minute, like sticks of sealing wax.

"Why, it's impossible to carry that to Camden Town," said Scrooge. "You must have a cab."

The chuckle with which he said this, and the chuckle with which he paid for the turkey, and the chuckle with which he paid for the cab, and the chuckle with which he recompensed the boy, were only to be exceeded by the chuckle with which he sat down, breathless, in his chair again, and chuckled till he cried.

Shaving was not an easy task, for his hand continued to shake very much; and shaving requires attention, even when you don't dance while you are at it. But if he had cut the end of his nose off, he would have put a piece of sticking plaster over it and been quite satisfied.

He dressed himself "all in his best," and at last got out into the streets. The people were by this time pouring forth, as he had been them with the Ghost of Christmas Present; and walking with his hands behind him, Scrooge regarded everyone with a delighted smile. He looked so irresistibly pleasant, in a word, that three or four good-humored fellows said, "Good morning, sir! A Merry Christmas to you!" And Scrooge said often afterward, that of all the blithe sounds he had ever heard, those were the blithest in his ears.

He had not gone far, when coming on toward him he beheld the portly gentleman who had walked into his counting house the day before and said, "Scrooge and Marley's, I believe?" It sent a pang across his heart to think how this old gentleman would look upon him when they met, but he knew what path lay straight before him and he took it.

"My dear sir," said Scrooge, quickening his pace and taking the old gentleman by both hands. "How do you do? I hope you succeeded yesterday. It was very kind of you. A Merry Christmas to you, sir!"

"Mr. Scrooge?"

"Yes," said Scrooge. "That is my name, and I fear it may not be pleasant to you. Allow me to ask your pardon. And will you have the goodness—" Here Scrooge whispered in his ear.

"Lord bless me!" cried the gentleman, as if his breath were taken away. "My dear Mr. Scrooge, are you serious?"

"If you please," said Scrooge. "Not a farthing less. A great many back payments are included in it, I assure you. Will you do me that favor?"

"My dear sir," said the other, shaking hands with him. "I don't know what to say to such munifi—"

"Don't say anything, please," retorted Scrooge. "Come and see me. Will you come and see me?"

"I will!" cried the old gentleman. And it was clear he meant to do it.

"Thank'ee," said Scrooge. "I am much obliged to you. I thank you fifty times. Bless you!"

He went to church, and walked about the streets, and watched the people hurrying to and fro, and patted the children on the head, and questioned beggars, and looked down into the kitchens of houses, and up to the windows, and found that everything could yield him pleasure. He had never dreamed that any walk—that anything—could give him so much happiness. In the afternoon he turned his steps toward his nephew's house.

He passed the door a dozen times before he had the courage to go up and knock. But he made a dash, and did it.

"Is your master at home, my dear?" said Scrooge to the girl. Nice girl! Very.

"Yes, sir."

"Where is he, my love?" said Scrooge.

"He's in the dining-room, sir, along with mistress. I'll show you upstairs, I you please."

"Thank'ee. He knows me," said Scrooge, with his hand already on the dining-room lock. "I'll go in here, my dear."

He turned it gently, and sidled his face in round the door. They were looking at the table (which was spread out in great array); for these young housekeepers are always nervous on such points, and like to see that everything is right.

"Fred!" said Scrooge.

Dear heart alive, how his niece by marriage started. Scrooge had forgotten, for the moment, about her sitting in the corner with the footstool, or he wouldn't have done it, on any account.

"Why, bless my soul!" cried Fred. "Who's that?"

"It's I. Your Uncle Scrooge. I have come to dinner. Will you let me in, Fred?"

Let him in! It is a mercy he didn't shake his arm off. He was at home in five minutes. Nothing could be heartier. His niece looked just the same. So did Toper when he came. So did the plump sister when she came. So did every one when they came. Wonderful party, wonderful games, wonderful unanimity, wonderful happiness!

But he was early at the office next morning. Oh, he was early there. If he could only be there first and catch Bob Crachit coming late! That was the thing he had set his heart upon.

And he did it; yes, he did! The clock struck nine. No Bob. A quarter past. No Bob. He was full eighteen minutes and a half behind his time. Scrooge sat with his door wide open, that he might see him come into the tank.

His hat was off before he opened the door, his comforter too. He was on his stool in a jiffy, driving away with his pen, as if he were trying to overtake nine o'clock.

"Hallo," growled Scrooge, in his accustomed voice as near as he could feign it. "What do you mean by coming here at this time of day?"

"I am very sorry, sir," said Bob. "I am behind my time."

"You are!" repeated Scrooge. "Yes, I think you are. Step this way, sir, if you please."

"It's only once a year, sir," pleaded Bob, appearing from the tank. "It shall not be repeated. I was making rather merry yesterday, sir."

"Now, I'll tell you what, my friend," said Scrooge. "I am not going to stand this sort of thing any longer. And therefore," he continued, leaping from his stool and giving Bob such a dig in the waistcoat that he staggered back into the tank again, "and therefore I am about to raise your salary!"

Bob trembled, and got a little nearer to the ruler. He had a momentary idea of knocking Scrooge down with it, holding him, and calling to the people in the court for help and a straight waistcoat.

"A Merry Christmas, Bob!" said Scrooge, with an earnestness that could not be mistaken, as he clapped him on the back. "A merrier Christmas, Bob, my good fellow, than I have given you for many a year! I'll raise your salary and endeavor to assist your struggling family, and we will discuss your affairs this very afternoon, over a Christmas bowl of smoking bishop, Bob! Make up the fires and buy another coal scuttle before you dot another i, Bob Cratchit!"

Scrooge was better than his word. He did it all, and infinitely more; and to Tiny Tim, who did not die, he was a second father. He became as good a friend, as good a master, and as good a man, as the good old city knew, or any other good old city, town, or borough, in the good old world. Some people laughed to see the alteration in him, but he let them laugh, and little heeded them, for he was wise enough to know that nothing ever happens on this globe, for good, at which some people did not have their fill of laughter in the outset; and knowing that such as these would be blind anyway, he thought it quite as well that they should wrinkle up their eyes in grins, as have the malady in less attractive forms. His own heart laughed; and that was quite enough for him.

He had no further intercourse with Spirits, but lived upon the Total Abstinence Principle, ever afterward; and it was always said of him, that he knew how to keep Christmas well, if any man alive possessed the knowledge. May that be truly said of us, and all of us! And so, as Tiny Tim observed, God Bless Us, Every One!

The Elves and the Shoemaker

BY THE BROTHERS GRIMM

THOUGH JACOB AND WILHELM GRIMM DEVOTED THEIR LIVES TO THE STUDY OF LITERATURE, THEY NEVER ACTUALLY WROTE ANY OF THE STORIES THAT WON THEM WORLD RENOWN. THE TALES THAT MADE THEM FAMOUS, *DER KINDER-UND HAUSMARCHEN* (*THE CHILDREN AND THE HOUSE OF FAIRY TALES*) WERE COLLECTED FROM THE EUROPEAN FOLKLORE AND LEGENDS OF THE TIME. WHILE *THE ELVES AND THE SHOEMAKER* STANDS ON ITS OWN AS A FAIRY TALE, IT IS ALSO AN EXAMPLE OF HOW AN ACT OF SELFLESS GIVING HAS THE POWER TO CHANGE LIVES FOR THE BETTER.

Once upon a time there was a poor shoemaker. He made excellent shoes and worked quite diligently, but even so he could not earn enough to support himself and his family. He became so poor that he could not even afford to buy the leather he needed to make shoes; finally he had only enough to make one last pair. He cut them out with great care and put the pieces on his workbench, so that he could sew them together the following morning.

"Now, I wonder," he sighed, "will I ever make another pair of shoes? Once I've sold this pair I shall need all the money to buy food for my family. I will not be able to buy any new leather."

That night, the shoemaker went to bed a sad and distraught man.

The next morning, he awoke early and went down to his workshop. On his bench he found an exquisite pair of shoes! They had small and even stitches, formed so perfectly that he knew he couldn't have produced a better pair himself. Upon close examination, the shoes proved to be made from the very pieces of leather he had set out the night before. He immediately put the fine pair of shoes in the window of his shop and drew back the blinds.

"Who in the world could have done this service for me?" he asked himself. Even before he could make up an answer, a rich man strode into his shop and bought the shoes—and for a fancy price.

The shoemaker was ecstatic; he immediately went out and purchased plenty of food for his family—and some more leather. That afternoon he cut out two pairs of shoes and, just as before, laid all the pieces on his bench so that he could sew them the next day. Then he went upstairs to enjoy a good meal with his family.

"My goodness!" he cried the next morning when he found two pairs of beautifully finished shoes on his workbench. "Who could make such fine shoes—and so quickly?" He put them in his shop window, and before long some wealthy people came in and paid a great deal of money for them. The happy shoemaker went right out and bought even more leather.

For weeks, and then months, this continued. Whether the shoemaker cut two pairs or four pairs, the fine new shoes were always ready the next morning. Soon his small shop was crowded with customers. He cut out many types of shoes: stiff boots lined with fur, delicate slippers for dancers, walking shoes for ladies, tiny shoes for children. Soon his shoes had bows and laces and buckles of fine silver. The little shop prospered as never before, and its proprietor was soon a rich man himself. His family wanted for nothing.

As the shoemaker and his wife sat by the fire one night, he said, "One of these days, I shall learn who has been helping us."

"We could hide behind the cupboard in your workroom," she said. "That way, we would find out just who your helpers are." And that is just what they did. That evening, when the clock struck twelve, the shoemaker and his wife heard a noise. Two tiny men, each with a bag of tools, were squeezing beneath a crack under the door. Oddest of all, the two elves were stark naked!

The two men clambered onto the workbench and began working. Their little hands stitched and their little hammers tapped ceaselessly the whole night through.

"They are so small! And they make such beautiful shoes in no time at all!" the shoemaker whispered to his wife as dawn rose. (Indeed, the elves were about the size of his own needles.)

"Quiet!" his wife answered. "See how they are cleaning up now." And in an instant, the two elves had disappeared beneath the door.

The next day, the shoemaker's wife said, "Those little elves have done so much good for us. Since it is nearly Christmas, we should make some gifts for them."

"Yes!" cried the shoemaker. "I'll make some boots that will fit them, and you make some clothes." They worked until dawn. On Christmas Eve the presents were laid out upon the workbench: two tiny jackets, two pairs of trousers, and two little woolen caps. They also left out a plate of good things to eat and drink. Then they hid once again behind the cupboard and waited to see what would happen.

Just as before, the elves appeared at the stroke of midnight. They jumped onto the bench to begin their work, but when they saw all the presents they began to laugh and shout with joy. They tried on all the clothes, then helped themselves to the food and drink. Then they jumped down, danced excitedly around the workroom, and disappeared beneath the door.

After Christmas, the shoemaker cut out his leather as he always had—but the two elves never returned. "I believe they may have heard us whispering," his wife said. "Elves are so very shy when it comes to people, you know."

"I know I will miss their help," the shoemaker said, "but we will manage. The shop is always so busy now. But my stitches will never be as tight and small as theirs!"

That shoemaker did indeed continue to prosper, but he and his family always remembered the good elves who had helped them during the hard times. And each and every Christmas Eve from that year onward, they gathered around the fire to drink a toast to their tiny friends.

A Letter from Santa Claus

BY MARK TWAIN

CLEMENT MOORE WAS NOT THE ONLY FATHER WHO DABBLED IN CHRISTMAS WRITINGS TO PLEASE HIS CHILDREN. THE FATHER OF YOUNG SUSIE CLEMENS, SAMUEL LANGHORNE CLEMENS (A.K.A. MARK TWAIN), ONCE TOOK PEN IN HAND TO CRAFT AN UNFORGETTABLE CHRISTMAS OFFERING.

Palace of St. Nicholas In the Moon
Christmas Morning

My Dear Susie Clemens:

I have received and read all the letters which you and your little sister have written me by the hand of your mother and your nurses; I have also read those which you little people have written me with your own hands—for although you did not use any characters that are in grown people's alphabet, you used the characters that all children in all lands on earth and in the twinkling stars use; and as all my subjects in the moon are children and use no characters but that, you will easily understand that I can read your and your baby sister's jagged and fantastic marks without any trouble at all. But I had trouble with those letters which you dictated through your mother and the nurses, for I am a foreigner and cannot read English writing well. You will find that I made no mistakes about the things which you and the baby ordered in your own letters—I went down your chimney at midnight when you were asleep and delivered them all myself—and kissed both of you, too, because you are good children, well trained, nice mannered, and about the most obedient little people I ever saw. But in the letter which you dictated there were some words which I could not make out for certain, and one or two small orders which I could not fill because we ran out of stock. Our last lot of kitchen furniture for dolls has just gone to a very poor little child in the North Star away up in the cold country above the Big Dipper. Your mama can show you that star and you will say: "Little Snow Flake" (for that is the child's name), "I'm glad you got that furniture, for you need it more than I." That is, you must write that, with your own hand, and Snow Flake will write you an answer. If you only spoke it she wouldn't hear you. Make your letter light and thin, for the distance is great and the postage very heavy.

There was a word or two in your mama's letter which I couldn't be certain of. I took it to be "a trunk full of doll's clothes." Is that it? I will call at your kitchen door about nine o'clock to inquire. But I must not see anybody and I must not speak to anybody but you. When the kitchen doorbell rings, George must be blindfolded and sent to open the door. Then he must go back to the dining room or the china closet and take the cook with him. You must tell George

WHY DOES *Santa* WEAR RED?

he must walk on tiptoe and not speak—otherwise he will die some-day. Then you must go up to the nursery and stand on a chair or the nurse's bed and put your ear to the speaking tube that leads down to the kitchen and when I whistle through it you must speak in the tube and say, "Welcome, Santa Claus!" Then I will ask wheth-er it was a trunk you ordered or not. If you say it was, I shall ask you what color you want the trunk to be.

Your mama will help you to name a nice color and then you must tell me every single thing in detail which you want the trunk to con-tain. Then when I say "Good-by and a merry Christmas to my little Susie Clemens," you must say "Good-by, good old Santa Claus, I thank you very much and please tell that little Snow Flake I will look at her star tonight and she must look down here—I will be right in the west bay window; and every fine night I will look at her star and say, 'I know somebody up there and like her, too.'" Then you must go down into the library and make George close all the doors that open into the main hall, and everybody must keep still for a little while. I will go to the moon and get those things and in a few minutes I will come down the chimney that belongs to the fireplace that is in the hall—if it is a trunk you want—because I couldn't get such a thing as a trunk down the nursery chimney, you know.

People may talk if they want, until they hear my footsteps in the hall. Then you tell them to keep quiet a little while till I go back up the chimney. Maybe you will not hear my footsteps at all—so you may go now and then and peep through the dining-room doors, and by and by you will see that thing which you want, right under the piano in the drawing room—for I shall put it there.

If I should leave any snow in the hall, you must tell George to sweep it into the fireplace, for I haven't time to do such things. George must not use a broom, but a rag—else he will die someday. You must watch George and not let him run into danger. If my boot should leave a stain on the marble, George must not holystone it away. Leave it there always in memory of my visit; and whenever you look at it or show it to anybody you must let it remind you to be a good little girl. Whenever you are naughty and somebody points to that mark which your good old Santa Claus' boot made on the marble, what will you say, little sweetheart?

Good-by for a few minutes, till I come down to the world and ring the kitchen doorbell.

—Your loving Santa Claus
Whom people sometimes call "The Man in the Moon"

WHY DOES *Santa* WEAR RED?

christmas, a poet's pastime

From William Shakespeare to Henry Wadsworth Longfellow, some of the most important poets in history have written about Christmas. In this chapter you'll find some of the most unforgettable verse ever written in the holiday spirit. Whether you choose to read the selections aloud or enjoy them privately, you're sure to get a big dose of the spirit of the season!

The Oxen

by Thomas Hardy

Though most of his work focuses on characters in the fictitious Wessex County, Hardy also wrote about Christmas. In "The Oxen," Hardy puts to verse a centuries-old legend: that at midnight on the eve of Christ's birth, and every Christmas Eve thereafter, the oxen fall to their knees in honor of the Lord.

Christmas Eve, and twelve of the clock.
    "Now they are all on their knees,"
An elder said as we sat in a flock
    By the embers in hearthside ease.

We pictured the meek mild creatures where
    They dwelt in their strawy pen,
Nor did it occur to one of us there
    To doubt they were kneeling then.

So fair a fancy few would weave
    In these years! Yet, I feel,
If someone said on Christmas Eve,
    "Come; see the oxen kneel

"In the lonely barton by yonder coomb
    Our childhood used to know,"
I should go with him in the gloom,
    Hoping it might be so.

Christmas—1863

BY HENRY WADSWORTH LONGFELLOW

ALTHOUGH DESCRIBING A SPECIFIC CHRISTMAS DURING THE CIVIL WAR, LONGFELLOW STRESSES IN THIS POEM A THEME THAT IS PERTINENT TO EVERY ERA: EVEN THOUGH LIFE IS FULL OF HARDSHIP, THE GOODNESS OF GOD WILL ALWAYS PREVAIL.

I hear the bells on Christmas day
The old familiar carols play,
And wild and sweet,
The words repeat
Of peace on earth, good-will to men.

Then from each black, accursed mouth
The cannon thundered in the South;
And with that sound
The carols drowned
Of peace on earth, good-will to men.

It was as if an earthquake rent
The hearthstones of a continent,
And made forlorn
The household born
Of peace on earth, good-will to men.

And in despair I bowed my head,
"There is no peace on earth," I said,
"For hate is strong
And mocks the song
Of peace on earth, good-will to men."

Then pealed the bells more loud and deep;
"God is not dead, not doth He sleep;
The Wrong shall fail,
The Right prevail,
With peace on earth, good-will to men."

A Visit from Saint Nicholas

('Twas the Night Before Christmas)

by Clement C. Moore

ON CHRISTMAS EVE, 1822, DR. CLEMENT CLARKE MOORE UNVEILED WHAT IS ARGUABLY THE MOST POPULAR CHRISTMAS POEM OF ALL TIME, "A VISIT FROM SAINT NICHOLAS." ALSO KNOWN AS "THE NIGHT BEFORE CHRISTMAS," THE POEM WAS WRITTEN STRICTLY FOR THE ENJOYMENT OF MOORE'S CHILDREN, BUT A LISTENER PRESENT AT THE READING WAS IMPRESSED ENOUGH TO SEND THE POEM TO THE TROY SENTINEL, WHERE IT WAS PUBLISHED THE FOLLOWING DECEMBER.

'Twas the night before Christmas, when all through the house
Not a creature was stirring, not even a mouse;
The stockings were hung by the chimney with care,
In hopes that Saint Nicholas soon would be there;

The children were nestled all snug in their beds,
While visions of sugarplums danced in their heads;
And Mama in her kerchief, and I in my cap,
Had just settled our brains for a long winter's nap—

When out on the lawn there arose such a clatter,
I sprang from my bed to see what was the matter.
Away to the window I flew like a flash,
Tore open the shutters and threw up the sash.

The moon on the breast of the new-fallen snow
Gave a lustre of midday to objects below;
When what to my wondering eyes should appear,
But a miniature sleigh and eight tiny reindeer.

With a little old driver, so lively and quick
I knew in a moment it must be Saint Nick!
More rapid than eagles his coursers they came,
And he whistled and shouted and called them by name:

"Now, Dasher! Now, Dancer! Now, Prancer and Vixen!
On, Comet! On, Cupid! On, Donner and Blitzen!

WHY DOES *Santa* WEAR RED?

To the top of the porch, to the top of the wall!
Now dash away, dash away, dash away all!"

As dry leaves that before the wild hurricane fly,
When they meet with an obstacle, mount to the sky,
So up to the housetops the coursers they flew,
With a sleigh full of toys—and Saint Nicholas, too.

And then in a twinkling I heard on the roof
The prancing and pawing of each little hoof.
As I drew in my head, and was turning around,
Down the chimney Saint Nicholas came with a bound.

He was dressed all in fur from his head to his foot,
And his clothes were all tarnished with ashes and soot;
A bundle of toys he had flung on his back,
And he looked like a peddler just opening his pack.

His eyes, how they twinkled! His dimples, how merry!
His cheeks were like roses, his nose like a cherry;
His droll little mouth was drawn up like a bow,
And the beard on his chin was as white as the snow.

The stump of a pipe he held tight in his teeth,
And the smoke it encircled his head like a wreath.
He had a broad face and a little round belly
That shook, when he laughed, like a bowl full of jelly.

He was chubby and plump—a right jolly old elf;
And I laughed, when I saw him, in spite of myself.
A wink of his eye and a twist of his head
Soon gave me to know I had nothing to dread.

He spoke not a word, but went straight to his work,
And filled all the stockings; then turned with a jerk,
And laying his finger aside of his nose,
And giving a nod, up the chimney he rose.

He sprang in his sleigh, to his team gave a whistle,
And away they all flew like the down of a thistle;
But I heard him exclaim, ere he drove out of sight:
"Happy Christmas to all, and to all a good-night!"

A Christmas Carol

BY CHRISTINA ROSSETTI

99

CHRISTINA ROSSETTI IS ONE OF ONLY A VERY FEW POPULAR FEMALE POETS OF THE NINETEENTH CENTURY. HER POEM AND THE DICKENS CLASSIC SHARE NOT ONLY A TITLE BUT ALSO A REVERENCE FOR CHRISTMAS. THE POEM REMINDS US THAT IT IS THE DESIRE TO GIVE, AND NOT THE GIFT ITSELF, THAT IS THE ESSENCE OF THE CHRISTMAS SPIRIT.

In the bleak mid-winter
Frosty wind made moan,
Earth stood hard as iron,
Water like a stone;
    Snow had fallen, snow on snow,
    Snow on snow,
    In the bleak mid-winter
    Long ago.

Our God, Heaven cannot hold Him
Nor earth sustain;
Heaven and earth shall flee away
When He comes to reign;
In the bleak mid-winter
A stable-place sufficed
The Lord God Almighty
Jesus Christ.

Enough for Him, whom cherubim
Worship night and day,
A breastful of milk
And a mangerful of hay;
Enough for Him, whom angels
Fall down before,
The ox and ass and camel
Which adore.

Angels and archangels
May have gathered there,
Cherubim and seraphim
Thronged the air;
But only His mother
In her maiden bliss
Worshipped the Beloved
With a kiss.

What can I give Him
Poor as I am?
If I were a shepherd
I would bring a lamb,
If I were a Wise Man
I would do my part,—
Yet what I can I give Him,
Give my heart.

Bird of Dawning

BY WILLIAM SHAKESPEARE

WHAT WOULD A COLLECTION OF CHRISTMAS LITERATURE BE WITHOUT A CONTRIBUTION
FROM THE BARD HIMSELF? THIS EXTRACT, FROM ACT ONE, SCENE ONE OF HAMLET,
CONVEYS IN A FEW BRIEF LINES THE ESSENTIAL SACREDNESS OF THE SEASON.

Some say that ever 'gainst that season comes
Wherein our Saviour's birth is celebrated,
The bird of dawning singeth all night long;
And then, they say, no spirit dare stir abroad;
The nights are wholesome; then no planets strike,
No fairy takes, nor witch hath power to charm,
So hallow'd and so gracious is that time.

WHY DOES *Santa* WEAR RED?

Christmas and New Year Bells

by Alfred, Lord Tennyson

Alfred, Lord Tennyson held the esteemed post of Poet Laureate of England from 1850 until his death in 1892. "Christmas and New Year Bells" recalls the importance bells hold to the celebration of the Yule: ringing out the old, and ringing in the new.

The time draws near the birth of Christ:
The moon is hid; the night is still;
The Christmas bells from hill to hill
Answer each other in the mist.

Four voices of four hamlets round,
From far and near, on mead and moor,
Swell out and fail, as if a door
Were shut between me and the sound:

Each voice four changes on the wind,
That now dilate, and now decrease,
Peace and goodwill, goodwill and peace,
Peace and goodwill, to all mankind.

This year I slept and woke with pain,
I almost wish'd no more to wake,
And that my hold on life would break
Before I heard those bells again.

But they my troubled spirit rule,
For they controll'd me when a boy;
They bring me sorrow touch'd with joy,
The merry, merry bells of Yule.

Ring out, wild bells, to the wild sky,
The flying cloud, the frost light:
The year is dying in the night;
Ring out, wild bells, and let him die.

Ring out the old, ring in the new,
Ring, happy bells, across the snow:
The year is going, let him go;
Ring out the false, ring in the true.

Ring out the grief that saps the mind,
For those that here we see no more;
Ring out the feud of rich and poor,
Ring in redress to all mankind.

Ring out a slowly dying cause,
And ancient forms of party strife;
Ring in the nobler modes of life,
With sweeter manners, purer laws.

Ring out the want, the care, the sin,
The faithless coldness of the times;
Ring out, ring out my mournful rhymes,
But ring the fuller minstrel in.

Ring out false price in place and blood,
The civic slander and the spite;
Ring in the love of truth and right,
Ring in the common love of good.

Ring out old shapes of foul disease,
Ring out the narrowing lust of gold;
Ring out the thousand wars of old,
Ring in the thousand years of peace.

Ring in the valiant man and free,
The larger heart, the kindlier hand;
Ring out the darkness of the land,
Ring in the Christ that is to be.

WHY, DOES *Santa* WEAR RED?